FORTY
OF WHITE

My Amazing Antarctic Journey

GINNI BAZLINTON

WITHDRAWN

EXPLORE

HIGH LIFE HIGHLAND	
3800 16 0026298 8	
Askews & Holts	Sep-2016
B DAZ	£11.99

First published in 2016 by

EXPLORE BOOKS
26 Grosvenor Road, London, N10 2DS

www.exploretravelwriting.com
email: explorebooks@outlook.com

Copyright text © 2016 Ginni Balinton
Foreword copyright @ 2016 Sir Ranulph Fiennes

All rights reserved. No part of this publication
may be reproduced, stored in a retrieval system, or
transmitted, in any form or by any means, electronic,
mechanical, photocopying, recording or otherwise,
without the prior permission of the publisher.

The right of Ginni Bazlinton to be identified as the Author of
the Work has been asserted by the author in accordance with
the Copyright, Designs and Patents Act 1988.

For bulk and special sales please contact explorebooks@travelwriting.com

A catalogue record for this book is available
from the British Library
Cataloguing-in-Publication Data is available
from the Library of Congress

ISBNs: 978-1-911184-00-3 (paperback)
978-1-911184-01-0 (ePub)
978-1-911184-02-7 (mobi)

Typeset by JPO design and typesetting.
Maps by Simonetta Giori.

Printed and bound in Great Britain by TJ International Ltd, Padstow, Cornwall

CONTENTS

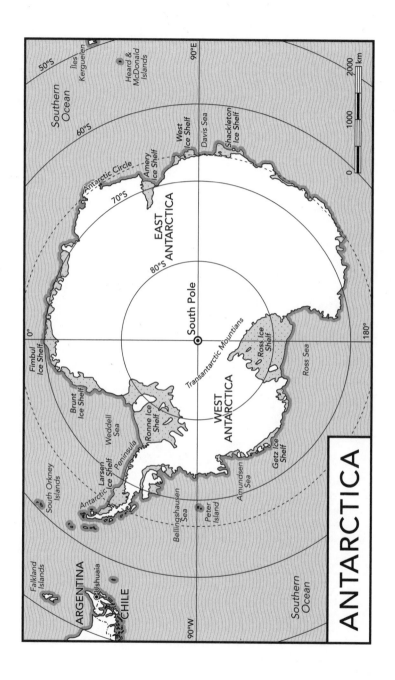

ANTARCTICA

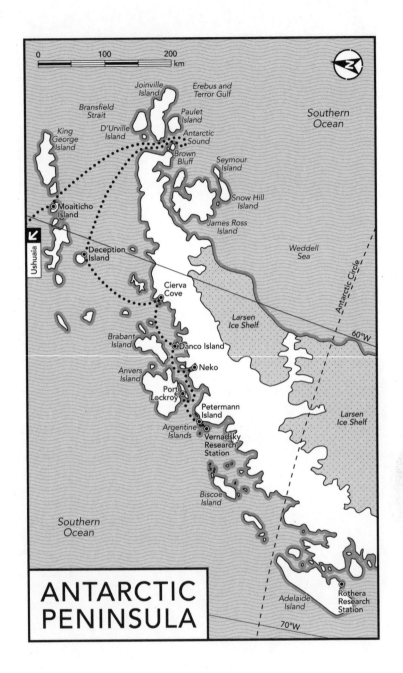

ANTARCTIC
PENINSULA

FOREWORD
by Sir Ranulph Fiennes

Forty Shades of White: My Amazing Antarctic Journey is the story of a grandmother who sets off alone to fulfil her childhood dream of going to the end of the world, totally unaware of the life-changing impact it would have on her. Her journey takes her to a unique continent that has changed very little in 55 million years. Virginia Bazlinton invites you to take a step back into childhood, that time of imagination, spontaneity and discovery, when the self is lost in the timeless immediacy of the moment. She enters a magical land which is still hiding many secrets; so far away from our daily lives that few of us know very much about this continent of superlatives. Over the years, many books have been written about Antarctica by scientists, TV presenters, explorers and travel journalists.

Forty Shades of White is different. It is Antarctica seen through the eyes of an ordinary member of the public. It clearly had a life-changing impact on the author, both enriching yet humbling her. Whether you pick up this book as background reading for a trip you propose making, or if you've already been there and want to compare your experience with others, it is a book worth reading.

I can fully understand Virginia's feelings, having led the first one-way crossing of Antarctica on the Transglobe Expedition 1979–82, and other later ventures on this continent. The uniqueness of this unspoilt land leaves one with a new sense of awareness – making Antarctica impossible to forget. This continent must be preserved, and this can only happen through knowledge and understanding of such an important place on our planet.

Sir Ranulph Fiennes, 2015

1. PROLOGUE

It rose out of the water like some giant prehistoric monster; it appeared to be smiling at us. It heaved its massive body up into the air, arching its back before diving back into the water with just its tail suspended like a weirdly shaped mushroom growing out of the sea. Then it disappeared back into the icy depths. I had no idea that a humpback whale could leave such an indelible imprint on my memory. But that was what Antarctica was like for me always taking me beyond what I knew. The decision to go was made spontaneously; I did not realise that the continent's sights and sounds like the humpback whale were to change the way I was to think about the world.

"You must be mad! Why on earth do you want to go to such a bitterly cold, remote place; there's nothing there and nothing to do?" That was the reaction I got from some of my friends. I couldn't answer why I wanted to go, it was just a spontaneous decision. My family however, thought it would be a wonderful adventure. They know I have an incurable travel bug and have to go off to some far-flung place from time to time. Their only comment was, "You won't do anything stupid will you?"

My academic achievements when I left school were sadly lacking. I used to spend a lot of my time daydreaming about being a ballerina; a status I didn't quite aspire to but I did make a living as a professional dancer in the theatre. My life treading the boards came to an end a couple of years after I got married with the arrival of my sons. I settled down to my new life as a wife and mother and continued to attend a weekly ballet class. Life was happy for fifteen years and then came the crash. Following divorce I found solace in education, it couldn't hurt me; it was up to me to work hard and succeed. I went to university and then taught English as a foreign language at an adult language school in Portsmouth.

One afternoon I was teaching a Spanish student named Manuel. He told me he didn't want to learn grammar, all he wanted to learn was new vocabulary, to speak and be corrected if he made a mistake. Having planned a lesson for him, I suddenly had to abandon it and think on my feet; well backside in this case. I sat poised with pen and paper at the ready and asked him to tell me about himself. He told me he was living in Chile and was the manager of a flying school in Santiago. He then described a train journey in the Andes, the longest mountain range in the world, going south from Santiago to a place called San Fernando. I was so engrossed with his vivid description of the terrain I don't recall even making one mark on the paper. Fortunately I was recording his lesson so we could analyse it later. I was hooked. I knew that as soon as my youngest son left home, Santiago was where I would go.

I spent eighteen months teaching in Santiago and before leaving for England I decided to spend three weeks in the far south of Chile and Argentina. On a Saturday in September I flew to Punta Arenas, the most southerly inhabited mainland place in the world. I booked into a *residencia* (a guest house) for two nights. I had hoped to leave for Ushuaia in Argentine Tierra del Fuego the next day but there were no buses on a Sunday. The next morning I woke up to heavy, overcast skies. Despite the terrible weather, I braved a walk along the seashore of the Magellan Strait, the graveyard of a good many ships that met their fate in the Southern Ocean. It was such a bleak, desolate place; a bone chilling cold wind lashed against me, and the rain, like sharp needles of ice, stung my face. I didn't see another human being anywhere; the atmosphere was forlorn and forgotten. I suppose it's only mad dogs and English grandmothers who go out in the morning wind and rain on the shores of the Magellan Strait.

There were a lot of shipwrecks along the shore, their great, rusting hulls belying their powerful, pioneering past. I felt rather sad as I walked along thinking of the poor people who'd perished in a distant, hostile land and freezing cold sea. As there was no other sign of life in the vicinity; I called out across the sea "You are not forgotten. I'm thinking of you." It was the only time in my life that I have felt lonely on my travels. I think my call was more to make me feel less alone than for the poor dead sailors who were unlikely to hear my voice. At the time I didn't know the following poem, but now I believe that maybe my voice was carried to the dead men on the wings of the albatross. The poem appears in Spanish on a plinth at Cape Horn with a sculpture of an albatross.

Soy el albatross que te espera	I am the albatross who waits
En el final del mondo	For you at the end of the world
Soy el alama olivida de los marinos muertos	I am the forgotten soul of the dead sailors
Que cruzaron el Cabo de Horno	Who crossed Cape Horn
Desde todos los mares de la tierra.	From all the seas of the earth.
Pero ellos no murieron	But they did not die
Em las furiosas,	In the furious waves,
Hoy vuelane en mis alas,	Today they fly on my wings,
Hacia la eternidad,	Towards eternity,
En la ultima grieta	In the last gust
De los vientos Antarctica.	Of the Antarctic winds.

(Sara Vial, December 1992)

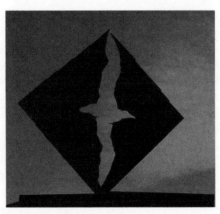

Albatross plinth at Cape Horn

Sara Vial was born and lived in Valparaiso, Chile. It was a place that inspired her work as a writer. She won the Gabriela Mistral Prize in 1976, and she was a friend of the late Chilean poet, Pablo

Neruda who won the Nobel Prize for literature in 1971. Gabriela Mistral was also a Chilean poet who won the Nobel Prize in 1945.

The following morning dawned sunny with occasional wisps of cloud in an otherwise azure sky. The bus left dead on time and took us along the coast of the Strait of Magellan, but in the opposite direction from my walk the day before. It was such a contrast from the desolate bleakness of the previous day. We soon arrived at the ferry that was to take us across the Strait of Magellan which separates the tip of the South American mainland from the islands of Tierra del Fuego. It was a lovely smooth crossing with dolphins doing acrobatics alongside the ship. After a journey of about half an hour, I finally set foot in the land of my childhood dreams. I felt as excited as a child on Christmas morning.

The Strait of Magellan is named after the Portuguese explorer, Ferdinand Magellan. He was the first European to circumnavigate the globe in 1519–22, building empires for Spain and Portugal in South and Central America. The Spanish had absolute control over the Strait and ships had to get permission from Spain if they wanted to sail down the Magellan Strait, which at the time appeared to be the only way of reaching the Pacific Ocean travelling east to west.

Back on the bus we continued our journey south along a dirt track road which was very slow going. The terrain consisted of endless flat pampas grass interspersed with rocky mounds and grazing sheep, and beautiful, brightly coloured birds darting away from the bus into the grassland. After a twelve-hour journey we arrived in Ushuaia at 7.30pm. and stopped at the Hostel Antarctica which looked very warm and inviting so I booked in for three nights. The reception counter was well stocked with very reasonably priced drinks. There were comfortable sofas around the room making it easy to meet and chat to other backpackers. A flight of stairs led up to an open kitchen area with two fridges and cooking facilities for guests. Breakfast was included in the price. There were four dorm rooms upstairs each with three bunk beds and there were private rooms on the ground floor opening up into a garden. There was also a library and free internet use. The staff were very friendly and went out of their way to be helpful.

The next morning I woke up to an unforgettable view across

The Beagle Channel

the Beagle Channel, which was named after HMS *Beagle*, the ship that Darwin sailed in. The sun was just rising and the sky was streaked with pink, green, blue and gold light, brushing the tops of the snow-capped mountains on the Chilean, south side of the channel. While I was having breakfast of coffee and scrambled eggs, a young woman came and joined me at the table. Her name was Sonja, she was from Germany and travelling alone like me. We discovered we'd been to a lot of the same countries including living in Japan. She'd given up her very good career in business to become a medical student. She asked me what I was going to do that day, I told her that I was hoping to go up a mountain to a glacier in the morning, and then take a boat trip down the Beagle Channel in the afternoon. She asked if she could join me and I readily agreed. I find that travelling alone is not the lonely experience a lot of people think it is, you actually meet a lot of interesting people. We spent a lovely morning going up the mountain on the chairlift then walking up to the glacier, sometimes knee deep or more in snow. Then in the afternoon taking a boat trip down the Beagle Channel enjoying the wildlife and scenery. The mountains on either side rose up straight out of the sea, topped with snow and forests. Fur seals and elephant seals were lolling on every rock that we passed and there were numerous sea birds. It was during this trip that I learnt that between November and March it was possible to get last minute cheap deals on ships going to Antarctica. Until then, Antarctica had never been a place I'd ever considered going to, let alone putting on my 'bucket list'. In fact, I'd never thought it was a place that was possible to visit by ordinary travellers; I really had very little interest in it either.

The seed of my Antarctic expedition was sown in the fertile soil of my imagination and watered by the spectacular images of the Beagle Channel; but it didn't take root immediately. I was actually surprised that it took root at all, but it was like a weed, inconspicuous, stubborn, and determined to survive in a way that I was not fully aware of at the time. It was born from no more than the knowledge that it was possible to get last minute cheap deals on ships going to Antarctica. Its conception was no more planned or desired than a pregnancy resulting from a one night stand. The seed blossomed into something that commanded closer attention and protection; it became the catalyst of a journey pushing further south than I'd ever been before. The word 'Antarctica' struck a chord in me that gradually resonated into a new experience. I had no idea of the impact that Antarctica would have on me.

When you were a child, did you use to read fantastic, adventure stories where anything could happen no matter how extraordinary? Maybe by pressing a secret panel you could be transported to a magical land. A place where there is no school, no homework and no grown-ups telling you what to do. You could act out the adventures of your fantasies with friends and become explorers discovering a myriad of interesting adventures. They say that childhood is the happiest time of our life, I suppose because a child tends to be so absorbed in the moment of play that the line between fantasy and reality becomes blurred for the duration of the game. As adults, it's hard to escape the harsh reality of our world; a world of commuting to work, traffic jams, job insecurity, increased crime, the threat of terrorist attacks and severe weather extremes causing death and devastation in some places. Wouldn't it be lovely to be like a child again and escape to a magical place of timeless adventure and be totally at one with the moment? A place where there are no cars, no streets lined with buildings, no shops so you don't need any money, no airports, no ports for ships, no world leaders squabbling over territory and the exploitation of diminishing resources. A place where nations work with each other for knowledge and the good of everything on the planet, rather than against each other for world domination. What would it be like if nobody owned the land we dwell on, or no single nation had greater power than the others? Is it possible to have a utopian world where we all work together and share our knowledge and discoveries? The answer of course is a resounding "NO!" To even suggest the possibility would invoke the reaction that I must be in Cloud Cuckoo Land, or on some recreational, hallucinatory drug.

I must confess that I have taken this 'drug'; I should warn you that it is highly addictive and so powerful that it has claimed the lives of many people and the hearts of many more. But it's a trip that takes you to a whole continent where all those utopian dreams come true. It's called 'Opposite Little Bear', it isn't a fictitious place, it really exists; its name comes from the Ancient Greek words, 'Anti-arktos', now known as Antarctica.

This journey has proved to be a life changing experience for me; a place that is not just a figment of a childish imagination, but an incredible reality, just you and this Antarctic nature. It's a continent that holds many secrets and a wealth of otherworldly experiences. Mirages and midnight sun; ice sculptures and volcanic fire; liquid gold light and blizzards; fertile seas and barren deserts; precipitous waves and mirror-calm seas; life and death – all this the ultimate contrast of extremes. Antarctica is unlike the rest of the planet as there are no indigenous people to claim sovereignty. It is so inhospitable that it would be impossible to live there permanently and build a thriving community.

When does a journey begin?

When does a journey begin? Is it when you shut your front door and put your luggage in whatever form of transport you are using? Is it when you board your plane, ship or coach? For me the seed of the first step of the journey was probably sown around the time that I was just stepping out of childhood into adolescence. I remember watching a documentary film on television about Tierra del Fuego which showed the life of the Fuegian Indians before the Europeans arrived. I found it so fascinating that the memory never left me. It portrayed a life where there was no outside interference, no advertisements telling you what you must look like or what new gadgets you must have. In Tierra del Fuego these things didn't seem to matter; you simply 'were'; a team working together for survival in nature's vibrant, but harsh world. Men hunted guanaco (members of the llama family) with spears, women dived into the icy waters to catch king crabs. They smothered themselves with seal blubber to keep out the cold. I remember seeing two little children aged about three playing naked in the snow. In the shelter of the tent, a woman gave birth and as soon as the umbilical cord was cut, the baby was taken outside and rolled in the snow before being handed back to the mother to suckle. It represented the most remote place in the world, a life so different from my own. An ultimate wilderness and an authentic way of being where nature led the way; it was so far removed from the manufactured, artificial world that I was trying to keep up with, I longed to go there. Since watching that documentary all those years ago the memory has never left me. Perhaps it was at the back of my mind when I listened to Manuel telling me about Santiago, and was still there many years later when I visited Ushuaia – saw the Beagle Channel – and heard that there was a route to another continent, a place even more remote from the modern world than Tierra del Fuego.

2. THE LAND OF FIRE

"The self having shed its attachments was free for the
strangest adventures. When life sank down for a moment,
the range of experience seemed limitless."
Virginia Woolf *To The Lighthouse*

Thirty-six thousand feet below us the coast of Brazil is a mass
of rivers, gleaming in the glow of the approaching dawn as they
wind their way to the coast. They look like incandescent skeins of
silver thread spread out in one of nature's repeated patterns, like
blood vessels flowing out into a dark body of water at the Atlantic
Ocean. I can see São Paulo lit up like a piece of jewellery, the lights
look like gems that have been scattered over the ground mapping
out the contours of the city. As we head south to Buenos Aires, the
sun is rising above the horizon and the terrain takes on a different
aspect, it is mainly flat pampas with a few small clusters of buildings. The time passes quite quickly and before long we are circling
the sprawling capital city of Argentina waiting for our landing
slot. We finally touch down at Ezeiza International Airport and
a crew member informs us that it's 7.00am. We all hastily change
our watches before disembarking.

Having retrieved my backpack and cleared immigration I go in
search of the shuttle bus ticket office. The shuttle bus runs between
the international airport and the domestic airport known rather
confusingly by two names, Aeroparque and Jorge Newbery. It is
situated on the coastal side of Buenos Aires. It's nice to stretch my
legs, but I'm very aware of being jet-lagged and alone in a large
unknown city in a far away continent in another hemisphere.
After wandering up and down the busy road for a while, I pluck
up the courage to ask someone the way to the shuttle bus ticket
office which fortunately is only a few minutes' walk away. The

buses leave every half hour and I'm just in time to catch one that leaves at 8.30am, the bus journey takes an hour

Despite having seven hours to wait before my flight on to Ushuaia, I am able to check my backpack in as soon as I arrive. What a relief as it's nearly as big as me and very heavy. The airport is just across the road from a milk chocolate coloured sea, the mouth of the River de la Plata. I am hot and tired and would love to wallow in cool water, but the murky brown colour isn't the least bit inviting. How strange it feels to leave home on a cold winter's day in February and less than twenty-four hours later arrive in Buenos Aires on a summer's day. What happened to spring? I've only dozed off for a short time; a whole season is a large chunk of time to lose in a life that is advancing too rapidly these days. Sitting outside for several hours waiting for my connecting flight to Ushuaia, I soon forget the loss of the end of winter as I enjoy the sun on my skin, much better than the bleak cold wind of February in England. Only seven hours to go until my departure to Ushuaia, but time passes quite quickly, and having dozed off for a couple of hours on a bench under a tree, it's soon time to go to the boarding gate.

Flying along the Beagle Channel, I feel as if I am following the flight of a condor. The mountains look beautiful in the evening light. They stretch in every direction as far as the eye can see. The crowns of the high ones are still covered in snow, but below the snow line the melting snow has left bare rock glistening in the setting sun. It looks as if a hairdresser has put a cape around the shoulders of the mountains and shaved the area below the crown so it's completely bald, just a white skullcap on the top. The lower slopes are covered with lush vegetation. A thrill of excitement and anticipation shoots through me. I hope I'll be sailing back down here in a few days time. It all looks so calm and peaceful, the rays of the setting sun are painting a gentle glow of burnished gold light over the mountains and sky, making a lie of the stories I've heard of the ferocious elements that lash the nearby Cape Horn, a notorious piece of land that has brought death to so many mariners. As we near Ushuaia the plane is getting lower and lower, and it seems as if we're coming down in the water; then I feel the comforting thud of the wheels touching the ground. The airport runway is a long strip of land in the channel running parallel to the shore, to which it is joined at the terminal. I assume it must be man-made, but I'm told it is natural land.

Tierra del Fuego means land of fire; it was named by the Portuguese explorer, Ferdinand Magellan, because of all the camp fires which the native Indians had to keep permanently lit. It is made up of hundreds of islands of various sizes lying off the southern coast of South America. The largest is Isla Grande where we've just landed. The taxi drops me off at Hostel Antarctica, where I'd stayed on my previous trip to Ushuaia. At the reception counter, which is also the bar, I give my name to the receptionist and tell her I don't know how long I'll be staying as I'm hoping to get a ship to Antarctica. The receptionist, Marianne, points to a notice on the counter:

ANTARCTICA
28th February – 8th March
THE AKADEMIK SHOKALSKIY
~~US$4,500~~ - US$4,000

I thank Marianne and say I'll think about it tomorrow. There's a young man sitting at the bar, he starts talking to me. He introduces himself by saying "Hi, my name's Darren, I'm from Canada." I reply "I'm Ginni from England." The conversation continues: "Are you travelling alone?"– "Yes, are you?"–"Yes, I'm leaving the day after tomorrow and want to have a king crab dinner before I leave Ushuaia. Do you want to come with me?"– "Not tonight, I just want to sleep."– "What about tomorrow night?"– "Yes, OK, see you tomorrow, goodnight!" I'm not in the habit of making dates with strange young men who I know nothing about other than their name and nationality, but there's something about travelling that makes me do things I wouldn't dream of doing at home. Also Darren seems like a nice young guy who probably feels more comfortable asking an older woman to go with him. A young woman of his own age might have thought it was a 'pick up'.

It's all Akademik

After a good night's sleep and breakfast I go into the town to see what ships and prices are on offer in the numerous travel agents dotted around the main street, Avenida San Martin. To my disappointment, all the trips advertised are for 21 days and are quite expensive. Just one travel company has the *Professor Shokalskiy* on offer for US$5,000; it is exactly the same date and same ship as the one advertised in the hostel. The only difference is the price and the word professor rather than Akademik. I'm a bit concerned about these two words; they seem a bit pretentious for the name of a ship. Then I reason that I've come all this way to Tierra del Fuego with the sole intention of going to Antarctica—how can I pass up such an opportunity because of some stupid reasoning about a word in the name of a ship? My childhood spirit of adventure kicks in US $1,000 more is a lot to pay, so unable to resist the call of the little white voices of Antarctica, I rush back to the hostel and tell Marianne I want to book it.

Marianne puts me in touch with a girl named Ana at a travel company called Canal, which I find tucked away in a side street. Ana is very helpful and chatty, her English is excellent. She tells me that she went to Antarctica in November of the previous year. She says that it was such an amazing experience she'd go back like a shot if she got the opportunity. I spend well over an hour booking it. I don't know if my insurance includes an air ambulance or not. Apparently it's compulsory on a voyage to Antarctica. Despite Ana's glowing opinion about Antarctica, the necessity of an air ambulance makes me feel even more ill at ease wondering what on earth could happen. My mind wanders back to the stories I've read about Scott and Shackleton's expeditions to Antarctica leading to frostbite and worse still, death in the case of Scott. Yes, I am covered for an air ambulance. It's full steam ahead and time to get over my irrational fears. Ana gives me some information about the leaders of our expedition. As soon as I read their biographies I realise why the word Akademik has been used. They are all professors, doctors, and highly educated in their academic fields, and veterans of numerous Antarctic expeditions. Not that that has anything to do with the name of the ship. There are a number of Russian ships that take passengers to the Polar regions, they were originally built for exploration work and were named after top Russian scientists. The *Akademik Shokalskiy* was built for polar and oceanographic research and was named after a Russian oceanographer named Shokalskiy; so she too is an academic in her own right. She is small with room for only 48 passengers, ice-strengthened and capable of reaching nooks and crannies that larger ships can't. I know I have done the right thing in booking her.

While Ana is completing all the paperwork for my trip, one of the other travel agents, a young man, tells me that the word Ushuaia originated from the native Indian name for this part of the Beagle Channel – 'ooshwhya' which means 'Bay Penetrating West'. I'm fascinated by this interesting and beautiful part of the world and eager to hear more of its intriguing past. Fortunately it's a quiet time at the travel agent's so I am rewarded by him telling me a story about my own British history in the area regarding Captain Robert Fitzroy and Charles Darwin. Fitzroy first sailed to Tierra del Fuego on HMS *Beagle,* carrying out hydrographical surveys of the area in 1828. When he saw the primitive existence of the local inhabitants he was shocked and considered them to be savages as they had long flowing hair and were naked. He decided to take a few of them hostage and take them to England in order to 'civilise' them by teaching them English, to dress respectably, learn good manners and eat with a knife and fork, and, most importantly to teach them to become good Christians. The idea was that they would be returned after several years in the hope that they would, in turn, 'civilise' the others in their tribe.

Initially Fitzroy took three women and six children hostage on his ship. Despite being some distance from land, all the prisoners escaped over the side except one girl of about nine years old who was very happy to stay. They named her 'Fuegia Basket'; the name had something to do with a basket belonging to a crew member on HMS *Beagle*. Fitzroy and the crew became very fond of the child; she was very quick to learn English and adapt to her new way of life. A short time later a young man willingly boarded the ship and was named 'York Minster' after the location where he joined the ship. York Minster was the name the ship's crew

15

gave to a sheer volcanic cliff rising out of the sea which reminded them of the cathedral in York. The next to join the little band of indians was 'Boat Memory', named after a whaleboat that the crew had been building when they were attacked, this man was the last link they had with the boat. As the ship continued her journey down the channel, they were intercepted by a group of Indians in canoes. They were not hostile, but selling fish and seal skins. Fitzroy wanted one of their men to join the ship and be taken to England with the three people he'd already taken aboard. A boy volunteered and Fitzroy gave his mother and father a few pearl buttons as payment, the newcomer was named 'Jemmy Button'. They spent four years in England during which time they acquired all the skills required of them. They were even presented to Queen Victoria at court. After the abolition of slavery, the capture of natives in far-flung places in the world had become common practice by Europeans; they had a growing fascination for 'wild' native peoples from exotic lands, as objects of curiosity. Later that curiosity for the exotic and the wild turned to plants and wild animals that were captured for their skins and as pets.

Just as they were about to be returned to Tierra del Fuego, Boat Memory died of smallpox. The other three Indians returned safely to their homeland on HMS *Beagle* under the command of Fitzroy and accompanied by Charles Darwin, who wanted to study the natural world of the area. It was a revelation to me that I was standing on the soil of the hallowed place where Darwin's interest, and detailed logging of his discoveries of nature, may have led to *The Origin of Species*. I hadn't even started my expedition to Antarctica and already I was experiencing that WOW feeling.

Also on board the *Beagle* was the Reverend Richard Matthews who, following the successful 'education' of the four Indians planned to establish a Christian mission on the shores of the Beagle Channel. At first things went well, so Captain Fitzroy and Darwin left Matthews to get on with his good work while they set off to explore more of the area. On their return they found that all was far from well in the mission: the Indians didn't take kindly to the Reverend Matthews's good intentions. He had personal items stolen, but worse than that, he was intimidated day and night by the locals—his life was intolerable. Fearing for his safety, he left

Tierra del Fuego with Fitzroy and Darwin. But that is not the end of story. A young man named Thomas Bridges enters the scene —the origin of his name is an interesting tale. His life had not started out too well; he was an orphan who had been found under a bridge in Bristol by the Reverend Despard. He had no identification other than the letter 'T' on his clothes. The combination of the bridge and letter T gave Despard the idea of the name Thomas Bridges.

In 1868 Bridges and his newly wedded wife, arrived on the shores of the Beagle Channel in the hope of opening a Christian mission, despite the failure of Reverend Despard and the fact that no white man had ever survived there before. With the help and support of his wife, they successfully set up a mission and built a voluntary refuge for the native Indians. It was called Harberton after the name of the village in Devon in England where he and his wife had married. He devoted his life to working with the Yamana Indians and eventually gave up trying to convert them to Christianity in favour of protecting them from white man's persecution in the form of the recently arrived sheep farmers settling in the area. He compiled a 30,000 word dictionary of the Yamana language into English. He died in 1898 and his son Lucas continued his work. Lucas was fascinated by the local culture, to the point of living and hunting as one of them and taking part in their magic rituals as well as getting involved in their blood feuds. Apart from the latter two things, Lucas was a man after my own heart. It was their culture that had appealed to me so strongly in that TV documentary I watched as a child. The old mission is now the Harberton Estancia, which is 87 kilometres east of Ushuaia, and is the oldest estancia in Tierra del Fuego, built in 1886 on a narrow peninsula on the Beagle Channel. It is a farmstead run by Thomas Bridges's great grandson, Tommy Goodall and his wife Natalie, and is open to the public for visits.

It is thought that the origin of the Fuegian Indian tribes had their roots in Asia about 14,000 years ago and crossed the Bering Strait to North America, before making their way down to the tip of South America. At the time of Fitzroy and Darwin's visit to the Beagle Channel, there were four groups of Indians: the Sek'nam, who inhabited the northern and central parts of Tierra del Fuego; the Alacalufs, who were nomadic and mainly travelled in canoes searching for shellfish, only coming on land to make shelters from branches covered by grass; the Haush, the oldest and smallest tribe, who were forced to the east of Isla Grande by the Selk'nam and another the afrementioned Yamana who lived on the shores of the Beagle Channel at what is now Harberton Estancia.

A European settlement was established in Ushuaia in 1870. The Argentineans were concerned about the growing British presence and set up a penal colony in Ushuaia to gain control of the area. At that time there was a population of about ten thousand Indians. Now, thanks to imperial power, diseases brought to the region by Europeans and slaughter of the natives, the tribes are extinct. Only a handful of mixed race Indians remain. I find it rather disconcerting to hear that the race of people, whose life-style at the end of the world that had so intrigued me in my youth, could be obliterated by colonial imperialism. Now, thanks to Thomas Bridges and his son Lucas, the Yamana language will at least survive.

Ana finally finishes all the paperwork, it has taken a long time, but it has been the most interesting travel booking I've ever made. Fired up with excitement, I decide to walk to the port. There's a massive luxury liner in the dock—I'm glad the *Akademik Shokalskiy* isn't as big or as luxurious as this one. On a luxury liner I'd feel like Cinderella every time I went into the dining room; the only clothing I have with me is my trekking gear. I doubt that a fairy godmother would appear over the side of the ship and wave a magic wand over me to make me look elegant, but I'm always prepared for the unexpected while I'm at sea. I remember the time King Neptune appeared over the side of the ship when I crossed the Equator in 1952 on a Union Castle liner. He didn't wave a wand and make me look elegant; he gave me a certificate, but more of that event later.

In the evening I go down to the lounge to meet Darren before setting off for our king crab dinner and what turns out to be a rather bizarre evening. The restaurant is quite large and obviously very popular judging by the number of people dining there. We are shown to a table for two and given the menu. We choose our king crab dish and discuss what wine to have. We agree on a bottle of Argentinean Malbec. It is strange; we know nothing about each other except our names and nationalities. As a conversation opener I ask him where he's heading off to tomorrow. He answers, "I'm going to Valdez to meet an Italian girl I met a few months ago and have fallen in love with her. She's very beautiful and very clever, she can speak Japanese". I tell him I lived in Japan for over two years and can speak a little Japanese; I ask him if he wants to know how to say 'I love you' in Japanese. His eyes light up as he says, "yessssssss!" I tell him, "watashi wa anata o aishitemasu" and write it down syllable by syllable. He keeps repeating it until he can say it without reading it. Despite the age difference—he is twenty-five, I am sixty-two—conversation is easy and we laugh a lot. Darren is a gentle, outgoing person with a great sense of humour. There's something about travelling that can make a complete stranger seem like a close friend, and age has no barriers. You will always find some common ground when travelling and plenty of things to talk about. If we'd met at a party, we probably wouldn't have spoken to each other, let alone be so animated. The bottle of Malbec probably helps. Towards the end of the evening Darren excuses himself and gets up from the table and goes to the bar at the back of the restaurant; I assume he's asking for the bill. A few minutes later he returns to the table and sits down. I get up to go to the ladies room but Darren starts behaving very strangely and asks me not to go yet. He seems a bit flustered and I can't get any sense out of him. I put it down to too much wine, then I start to worry that he hasn't got any money and I'm going to have to pay his share of the bill as well as my own. A few minutes later a waiter comes to our table and places a chocolate ice cream cake with one lighted candle in front of me. With that, he and Darren start singing 'Happy Birthday' to me, quickly followed by the other diners in the restaurant joining in. I try to tell Darren it's not my birthday, but he quickly silences me. What a crazy way to end the evening. I thank everyone and Darren and we polish off the cake. On the way back to the hostel I ask Darren why he'd told the waiter it was my birthday. He replies "It's a sure way of getting a free dessert."

The end of the world

Seventy per cent of the islands that make up the Tierra del Fuego archipelago belong to Chile; the other thirty per cent belong to Argentina. Ushuaia belongs to Argentina and is on the main island of Isla Grande, situated on the northern shore of the Beagle Channel; it has a population of approximately 45,000. It is known as *El Fin del Mondo*, The End of the World. The Argentineans claim it is the most southerly city in the world.

The Hostel Antarctica has a well-stocked bookcase with a range of books in a number of different languages. There are well-known guide books, novels, and one that really catches my attention. It is a guide book about places to visit in Tierra del Fuego and how to get there. There are so many interesting places to go to, it's hard to choose, but there is one along the Beagle Channel that looks wild and safe; also it isn't too far away. Decision made, I take a bus eastward to the final stop where the small city of Ushuaia comes to an abrupt end and beyond which there is very little habitation other than the Harberton Estancia. It's a journey of about 45 minutes and the buses are every 30 minutes. Despite increased tourism, Tierra del Fuego is still a magical place. Just a short walk from the bus stop, I immediately find myself in a wilderness so beautiful it makes me catch my breath. The inviting waters of the Beagle Channel are gently lapping the shores of the silver, sandy beach. The sunlight glinting on the water seems to be drawing me towards it; I'm powerless to resist the temptation and paddle in water up to my knees. "Brrrr, cold!" When the pain penetrates through to the bone, it's time to say goodbye to the cold water and enjoy the warmth of the sand while I wait for my feet to dry.

There is an abundance of marine life in the area, so it's probably best to keep a distance. Antarctic fur seals and southern sea lions are taking up most of the space on the rocky outcrops along the channel. Antarctic fur seals are much smaller than sea lions. Males weigh about 440 lbs, females weigh 110 lbs. They are sociable animals, but have been known to bite humans, who they can out run on land. In the past they were hunted to near extinction. It is the southern sea lions lolling around on the beach that fascinate me most, they look like overweight sumo wrestlers who've over indulged in the good life and are too bloated to move. Males weigh 770 lbs and females weigh 310 lbs. They are so close together that they sometimes end up rolling over onto the pups and squash them. Pups are born in December and mating begins again in January and continues until February. The males spend most of this time fighting and having sex. (Not so different from some humans!) At the end of this period they are exhausted and thin, so spend the next six months sleeping and eating. They aren't taking any notice of me as I walk along the beach, but I'm not going to take any risks and go too close to them, although as it's the end of February, their indolence must mean the mating game has ended. I defer to their great strength and aggressive nature, so decide to clamber up a steep embankment and stroll along a narrow path. A visual display of colour is spread out on one side of the path; the mountains reaching up to the clear blue sky to my left, the Beagle Channel glittering invitingly on my right. I ignore it; I'm not going to get my feet burnt twice, or rather frozen in this case.

Humans and seals are not the only summer visitors to the Beagle Channel, magellanic penguins, also known as jackass penguins because of their call (which sounds like an ass braying) are staying in their 'holiday homes' to make the most of the good weather. They nest by burrowing into the ground near the sea, a bit like shallow rabbit holes. It seems strange to see black and white penguins' heads poking out of what look like rabbit holes, but as soon as I go near them, they disappear into the depths of their underground homes.

The flora in Tierra del Fuego is surprisingly diverse, given its proximity to Antarctica. I wander through evergreen forests of beech, including a dwarf deciduous form called lenga beech which is low-lying with leaves that blush red and gold in autumn; late March is the best time to experience the full glowing effect. The leaves in the trees, stirred by the soft breeze, sing their song of welcome in a whispering voice. A flash of red darts across my view and touches down on the branch of a small beech tree. It's about the size of a thrush, but rounder, with the most vivid red breast I've ever seen. It's a beautiful long-tailed meadowlark. It is soon joined by others, their breasts are the colour of sunset, their backs and wings are brown. I'm amazed at the colour and variety of plant life; lupins of every hue nod to me in the light breeze as I pass. There are gentians, saxifrage, fuchsias, mountain sorrel, sea-pinks, anemones and orchids. The wild flowers are wafting their perfume on the light breeze and attracting colourful butterflies; everything seems to be communicating with me. It's as if they are smiling at me and reaching out to make physical contact as I pass by. I wonder if any scientists have ever tried to discover if plants can radiate wave lengths that connect with us, or if we give off vibrations that connect with plants. I don't need human company with all these friends within nature being so welcoming. I feel as if I'm the only person in the world, but it isn't a lonely feeling as it had been on that cold blustery day in Punta Arenas. Here, the sky is azure, the plant life radiating a vibrancy and friendliness that seems almost like a welcome greeting. As I walk along I feel so free; so much a part of nature not just an observer, but connected to it, which we all are of course. I want to build a shelter and spend a few days in this peaceful paradise, but I think I'd be terrified when the night's blackness sweeps the blue sky away. I don't think the wild animals in Tierra del Fuego would be as kind to me as the plants. I'm sure I'd make a tasty meal for a hungry, prowling Puma.

When I am close to nature, I see my childhood spread out across a wonderland of freedom, innocence, discovery and time-lessness. A state of simply being; an important lesson in life that cannot be taught, it can only be experienced. As a child I lived in Hayling Island which was then a semi-rural area. My sister and our friends used to play in the fields and woods. We knew the name of every wild flower and every bird. We could also identify the species of bird by the eggs in the nest, only if the mother wasn't sitting—we knew we mustn't touch the eggs as she might abandon them. There were ditches along the sides of the lanes to drain the rainwater. We used to build bridges across the ditches from wind-blown broken off tree branches by laying them across the ditch from the top of one bank to the bank on the opposite side. They were never particularly strong, but then we weren't particularly heavy. We didn't care if we fell in the ditch; it was all part of the fun of adventure. Fortunately we all had parents who thought it was healthier and better for us to play outside than in. We also built hideouts in the undergrowth. We all worked together and co-operated, looking out for each other. It was a time of creativity, using our imagination and free expression. The wildness of the hills and shoreline of the Beagle Channel remind me of my childhood games, a throwback to a more primitive existence hidden deep inside us; our very survival instincts. Sadly 'civilisation' has led to us becoming alienated from nature. Sigmund Freud said "The idea of civilisation too, has long been opposed to wilderness. The principle task of civilisation is to defend against nature." Today it is nature that needs defending against civilisation.

I think a lot of our childhood games are a throwback to a more primitive existence. Once when I was looking after my grandchildren, four-year-old James and six-year-old Sophia, they wanted to play hide and seek. Sophia came up with the idea of playing 'spooky hide and seek'. That meant hiding in the dark with no lights on at all, except in the kitchen where the person counting was standing before coming to seek for the hidden 'prey'. I stood in the kitchen and counted to twenty while James and Sophia went and hid in the living room. I found them both hiding behind the curtains at the French windows. Then they went in the kitchen to count while I hid; they finished counting and stood on the threshold of the living room; suddenly Sophia started to cry and say she didn't like it. That started James off too. At first I thought they were just pretending to be scared, but their crying soon turned to screaming and they were both shaking with fear when I rushed up to them and held them tightly. It made me think that in children the dormant genes are perhaps closer to the surface than in adults, and hide-and-seek is a game of predator and prey. As hunter-gatherers, we wouldn't have hunted at night.

As I walk back to the hostel, I'm halted in my tracks by a beautiful rainbow that appears out of nowhere, arcing across the mountains to the east. I take it to be a good omen: "Only a few more days to go till our voyage to Antarctica!"

The legend of Calafate

This mountainous area of ancient, jagged rock is filled with hidden treasures just waiting to be discovered. I book a trek to some ice caves and a glacier high up in the mountains. It's a beautiful day, very warm - 21°C, sunny with a clear blue sky. My guide's name is Daniel, he's from Buenos Aires but hates city life so he's come to one of the most remote areas in the south of South America. We drive through rugged scenery for about half an hour in a north easterly direction, eventually coming to a lodge where we stop to get a pair of rubber boots each, crampons and a packed lunch. Donning the boots we set off across a peat bog, passing a lot of ghostly, skeletal dead trees. Beavers, which were introduced to Tierra del Fuego from North America, cause the trees to die by gnawing at them to build dams and altering the course of the water by forming small lakes in which they build their lodges, which adds to the devastation. I inhale deeply as each footstep squeezes the musty aroma of the peat as we squelch our way across this unusual landscape. In places there are marshy pools of all the colours of the rainbow, their swirling shapes forming an abstract 'painting' on the ground. Daniel tells me it is natural oil oozing up from just below the surface. We pass a beaver's lodge

Boggy land on the way towards the ice caves

24

in the middle of a lake, it looks like a grey stick igloo floating on the uninviting water. We watch for a while and are rewarded by a beaver popping up from below the lodge and swimming purposefully to the bank to gather more sticks. Although I don't like the devastation they are causing to the environment, I am pleased to be able to watch them at work.

As soon as we pass the boggy land, we stop and put our walking boots back on. We leave our rubber boots under a tree. I'm sure we'll never find them again as the trees all look the same, so does the terrain. We walk through a beautiful forest of beech trees that have not been destroyed by beavers, and pass a milky looking, turquoise lake and river. Daniel says the water is safe to drink, he explains that the milky appearance is because the bottom of the lake is covered in finely ground up rock that has been worn down to powder by glacial action; no organisms are able to live in this kind of water, so it's pure. Of course I have to cup my hands and drink some, it tastes very gritty.

We walk on, stopping long enough to pick and eat some wild strawberries and calafate. Calafate is a native evergreen plant of the south of Chile and Argentina and is a symbol of Patagonia. It grows on a low bush and has small yellow flowers in summer and dark bluish/purple berries in autumn, a bit like a blueberry in appearance. The town in Argentine Patagonia was named Calafate after this plant. This is the first time I've eaten the real calafate fruit; it's probably the most famous fruit in Patagonia and Tierra del Fuego. There is a legend that anyone who eats the fruit of the calafate will return to the area. It doesn't have to be the actual fruit; it can be anything made from the fruit such as jam or ice cream. Needless to say on my first visit to El Calafate, I ate copious quantities of calafate ice cream. It was addictive! I've also boosted ice cream sales in Ushuaia as well. I know I will come back for a third time because now I've eaten the actual calafate fruit.

A couple of hours later we start hiking up quite a steep ascent slipping on scree and clambering over large boulders of granite, marble, calcium and iron. The terrain is like a kaleidoscope of autumn colours from all the minerals in the rocks. I wish we could stop and look at the exquisite patterns of the different minerals in the stones instead of stumbling over them—well I'm stumbling, Daniel isn't. The going gets really tough and I become painfully aware of how out of condition I am for this kind of trek, but stopping occasionally to admire the wonderful varied scenery makes it an enjoyable experience and gives me time to get my breath. We make it to the ice caves which are not as spectacular as the pictures indicated. I expect the pictures were taken in the winter and now it's the end of the summer. However, they are interesting and the trek is worth it. They consist of snow that has fallen during the winter, and as the layers have built up they've turned to ice through compression. The ice stretches across the boulders forming a ceiling between them, making an icy cave-like structure. In some places the ice is still very thick forming gleaming white and blue walls.

The glacier is another two-hour hike away, which means going at a faster speed than we've been walking at so far; my fault not Daniel's. I tell him I don't think I'll be able to make it to the glacier and back. He agrees, and makes me feel better by saying that a lot of people camp overnight at this point and set off for the glacier the next morning. We are running out of time and I know I'll enjoy the day more if I'm not pressured into having to rush. Also I've only worn crampons once before in my life when I climbed Volcán Villarrica in Chile and they kept falling off, so it will be even harder going for me than wearing only walking boots. We sit outside the entrance to one of the caves and eat our packed lunch; a somewhat surreal place to have a picnic.

We spend a bit more time exploring the ice caves before starting our descent. On the way back I paddle in the lake which is 5°C, but it makes my aching feet feel much better. It's lovely to walk along barefoot for a while and feel the soothing effect of the cool, damp grass on my feet, but I dread forcing my feet back into my walking boots. At the top of one of the mountains I notice an unusual, square turret shaped rock. Daniel tells me it is known as Laura's Molar. When he tells me that, I can see the strong resemblance to a molar. Apparently, Laura was the girlfriend of the first man to climb the mountain. I wonder if I'd be flattered if my boyfriend named a piece of square rock balanced precariously on the top of a mountain after one of my teeth. Perhaps he was a dentist. I wonder if there are any romantic stories about Laura and her lover. Thinking about it (further), perhaps having a rock on top of a mountain named after one of your teeth is rather romantic.

As we're looking skyward at Laura's Molar, we see one of South America's most iconic bird, the condor, a member of the vulture family. Despite their rather ugly appearance, with a wing span of over twelve feet and around seventeen-and-a-half pounds in weight, they look very graceful soaring high into infinity. I think the dirty-pink bare wattle on their heads with a long bare crest on their foreheads is very unattractive. Their coal black bodies and tail, and in particular their black wings, are quite graceful with splayed finger-like feathers along the wing edges.

We arrive back at the boggy ground. We, or rather Daniel, walk straight up to the tree where we've left our rubber boots without even a hint of hesitation that we are at the right tree. As we squelch our way back to the lodge, tired but happy, we see two more condors gliding above us. It is a memory I'll never forget.

When we get back to the lodge we have a lovely refreshing drink of yerba mate (pronounced *mattay*), an Argentinean green tea. It's followed a little later with a very welcome glass of red wine which makes me feel very relaxed and a bit sleepy. Then it's back to the hostel—I can hardly walk when I get out of Daniel's 4WD. I have a much needed shower and collapse into bed feeling very relaxed despite every part of my body aching. I am far too tired to bother rummaging in the fridge for something to eat. It has been a wonderful day with such varied terrain and wildlife, and I couldn't have wished for a friendlier, kinder more informative guide. I feel blissfully happy and content. I know that I will soon be sailing to Antarctica.

And we're off

Ushuaia is situated on the northern shore of the Beagle Channel surrounded by glaciated mountains whose jagged peaks rise to a level of 4,900 feet. The upper limit of vegetation is 1,640 feet. From this awe-inspiring setting we begin our trip to Antarctica. We've been told to meet at a point on the promenade at 4.00pm. where a coach will take us to the ship. When we board the coach we hand over our passports to Geoff Green, the expedition's leader.

As we get off the coach our passports are given back to us with a sticker telling us our cabin number: mine is 337. I find it easily and wait eagerly to meet my cabin mate. It's always quite an anxious time when you are going to be cooped up in the same cabin with a total stranger for the duration of the expedition. I don't have to wait long. Elizabeth, 'Libby' for short, walks in and we recognise each other instantly. We'd met in a shop in town when we were hiring rubber boots, waterproof trousers and other things. Libby is from Cape Town and is eleven months older than me. I am so pleased to be sharing a cabin with Libby—not only is she a very caring person, she is also very interesting. I ask her why she has chosen to come to Antarctica. She says that she's travelling round South America, and Ushuaia is her starting point. A few days ago she went into a travel agent in the main street to find out about interesting places to visit, they told her about a last minute cheap deal to Antarctica. She says she couldn't resist it.

As we unpack, we continue to get to know each other better. Our conversation flows easily. Many years ago she got her private pilot's licence and was a helicopter navigator as well. In October 1974 she was working for an aerial geophysical survey company searching for minerals when the plane she was flying in crashed. She received a compression fracture of her third lumber vertebra, three broken ribs, a badly bruised face and a punctured lung. There were three people in the aircraft, sadly one died. Libby and the pilot survived. He was able to walk and went to get help. Far from putting her off ever flying again, the crash spurred Libby on to get her commercial pilot's licence. Not content with that, since the accident, having been very active in sport, she has taken up long-distance trekking and hiking and is an adventurer and world traveller. She's a remarkable woman with grit, determination and a zest for life and exploration belying her age.

We are given a copy of the ship's itinerary: **Wednesday 28th February** – board our expedition vessel the *Akademik Shokalskiy* : Lifeboat Safety Drill: A champagne welcome toast. **Thursday 29th February** – cross the Drake Passage en route to Antarctica. **Friday 1st March** – 8.00am visit Paulet Island: 3.30pm make a landing on Brown Bluff. **Sunday 2nd March** – 8.15am arrive at Deception Island where we will attempt to land on the outside of the island and inside in Whaler's Bay: 2.30pm afternoon flexible depending on sea conditions. **Monday 3rd March** – 6.30am early morning landing on Danco Island: 10.00am land at Neko Harbour: 4.00pm arrive at Port Lockroy. **Tuesday 4th March** – 7.30am cruise down the Lemaire Channel: 9.15 am land at the Yalour Islands: 2.00pm land at the Ukrainian research station of Vernadsky. **Wednesday 5th March** – 7.45am arrive at Cuverville Island: 5.30pm head for the Melchoire Islands and then depart for

View from the stern

Ushuaia. **Thursday 6th March** – cross the Drake Passage. **Friday 7th March** – head north to Ushuaia. **Saturday 8th March** – Customs and Quarantine procedures completed: disembarkation in Ushuaia.

At 5.00pm. we all troop out on deck to watch our ship slip its mooring and head out into the Beagle Channel. All the passengers are fired up with exuberant anticipation for the adventure ahead. We're as excited as boisterous schoolchildren setting off on a long anticipated adventure into a world far removed from anywhere else on Earth. To port the views are of Ushuaia and the Argentinean side of Tierra del Fuego; to starboard the high mountains on the Chilean side dominate the skyline. Is it better to be on a high deck or a lower one? Bow or stern? Our childlike desire to try and see everything at once doesn't diminish as the ship glides out into the channel. The excitement and anticipation of things to come, a feeling that seems to be shared by all of us, is a great way of breaking the ice and getting to know each other.

Once we're well underway we all head back to the bar to be introduced to key members of the crew and the leaders of the expedition, all of whom are experts in their various fields and will be on hand to tell us not only about what we can expect to see, but also interesting facts to make our experience of Antarctica more enjoyable and informative. Education and interpretation are key elements of the expedition. 'Students on Ice', the company that has organised the expedition, has assembled an international team of scientists and polar experts whose experience and enthusiasm ensures that we will come away with a deeper understanding and appreciation of the Antarctic. Little did I know just what an amazing voyage of personal discovery and awakening it would be for me, and how it would shape my future life.

Safety of course is paramount. We are told about shipboard rules, particularly to always keep one hand free for the ship at all times. We go back on deck for lifeboat drill, a necessary but rather disconcerting affair. At least our lifeboats are covered over but I wouldn't want to spend any length of time in one of these boats in choppy seas; it would be like being thrown about in a box with no light inside and no view of what was outside, although it would be preferable to drowning. Apparently the lifeboats on *The Explorer*, which sank in Antarctica in November 2007, were all open to the elements and some people went into them wearing nothing more than their pyjamas. Fortunately they were all rescued very quickly, but they must have experienced a period of excruciating cold and fear.

The very important, serious stuff over with, it's time to lighten up as we all troop back to the bar for Captain Igor Kiselev's champagne welcome party. The champagne is flowing and conversation is easy. Everyone has interesting travellers' tales to tell, the more so as we are from all corners of the world. This is my first experience of travelling on a tourist ship and I am so pleased that the small number of passengers makes it easy to mingle with nearly everyone. Also I like the informality. Eventually the corks stop popping as it's time for dinner. There are two small dining rooms and we can sit where we like. I am very impressed with the choice of dishes on the menu and the quality of the food, all provided by the hands of our father and son team of two, Chilean chefs Alexandro and Jose.

After dinner everyone goes up on deck or on the bridge as we continue sailing down the Beagle Channel. The late evening sky is clear, the sun shows no sign of sinking below the horizon and its iridescent glow is in complete contrast to the dark cloak enveloping the waters of the channel. We are lucky to see numerous species of sea birds along the way; they are out hunting for their supper. Huge numbers of black-browed albatrosses are sitting in the water; the flat, calm conditions probably prevent them getting airborne. To take off they have to run along the surface of the water and be lifted into the air by an air current. Four hundred individuals have been counted so far within a very short distance of setting sail. (Not by me I might add!) I wouldn't even be able to start to count such a large flock of birds. They've been counted by Juan, our ornithologist. There are a lot more albatrosses further away, making it impossible to count, even for him. There are also some Magellanic penguins with their double-black breast bands on their white fronts; they are the only birds that I can so far identify having seen them on my walk along the Beagle Channel and in Otway Sound.

We pass Puerto Williams on the southern shore. It belongs to Chile and is technically the southernmost town in the world, but it is much smaller than Ushuaia. The journey down the Beagle Channel takes six hours; it remains light until about 10.00 pm. as the mountains are looming like dark shadows in the fading evening light. Dusk follows very quickly, the darkening sea is merging with the sky making the mountains barely visible as night descends on the 'End of the World'. We enter the waters of Cape Horn at around midnight. I put the patch behind my ear that Dr. Turner, my doctor in England, has given me to prevent sea-sickness. Despite feeling on a high with a sense of anxious anticipation as to what tomorrow might hold, I go to bed. We are entering the most treacherous sea in the world. It's farewell to 'civilisation'.

3. ANTARCTIC AIR AND WATER

"Some of us are over the seasickness stage
and no longer want to die."
A.E. Harbord on Shackleton's *Nimrod* expedition

I am not dreaming. I wake up to the realisation that I am being carried to another world. I can no longer make decisions as to where I will go, or how long I will stay. I am at the mercy of the ship's captain, the shipboard leaders, and in particular, we are all at the mercy of the elements. The journey has truly begun. I have no idea what to expect from this 'unknown' land, but I am soon to find out.

Antarctica is a continent of superlatives: it is the most remote place on earth, the most southerly and has the most severe climate of anywhere in the world. It is the windiest with average wind speeds of 67 miles per hour, but the wind can be up to 200 miles per hour. It is the coldest; the lowest temperature ever recorded was -89°C at the Russian station of Vostok. It's the driest, one of the most arid deserts in the world. That is hard to comprehend as the word 'desert' usually conjures up an image of endless sand and hot sun; Antarctica is a desert of endless snow. The dictionary entry defines a desert as a large area of land without water or trees, so it really is a desert, although paradoxically it contains 70 per cent of the world's fresh water, mainly in the form of ice. It contains 90 per cent of the world's ice and snow; 99 per cent of the land is covered in ice. It is home to the world's most southerly volcano, and is also the only pollution-free place on the planet.

It is the only continent where there are no pigeons—to many people that would be a bonus as they can be a nuisance. Pigeons are much maligned by many people, but they saw active service in the Second World War. Homing pigeons were used to drop messages to the Allies in occupied territories in the hope that the messages would not be found by the enemy. The Allies would reply to the sender and return their message back via 'pigeon secret agent'. Pigeons are seldom recognised for their bravery and commitments to the war effort, but for all we know they may well have helped to end the war.

Air and water are like dance and music: they are both movement and sound from energy. They can be a slow, gentle *lento*—seductive, enticing and full of promise, gliding like a skater across the ice, steady and smooth, radiating trustworthiness. But are they really a wolf in sheep's clothing? With a sudden change of tempo they can become *prestissimo* – fast, flamboyant, spontaneous and wild, sometimes ending in destruction and heartbreak.

After a very quiet, peaceful night's sleep, upon waking I'm aware of the ship rocking and rolling from side to side. I'm surprised at the strength of the motion. I hadn't felt any movement until I woke up. I'm not a good traveller on the sea, I'd rather be in it, so I'm surprised I wasn't disturbed during the night. Fortunately I'm sleeping athwartships, so sliding up and down in my bed is much less likely to cause seasickness than rolling from side to side I think. I get up and walk along the corridor to have breakfast and immediately understand why 'one hand for the ship at all times' has been drilled into us. I'm finding it quite difficult to stand up and walk in a straight line despite clinging to the railings with both hands. After a cup of coffee and a light breakfast I start to feel a bit queasy. I can't understand why as the ear patches are supposed to counterbalance the motion of the ship. We are told that our present position is 57° 26'S. I can neither visualise our position in the Southern Ocean, nor have any inkling as to whether it has any bearing on sea conditions. I assume the sea must be very rough. We've been warned that the Drake Passage is the most treacherous sea in the world so, it's no wonder many of us have succumbed to the motion.

We are given a copy of the Beaufort Scale that measures wind velocity and sea disturbance. Looking at it I guess we must be experiencing the higher end of the scale, gale force winds and 40 foot waves, as that would explain the reason why so many of us are being affected by the motion of the ship. I make my way up to the deck to get some fresh air. As I open the door I'm expecting to find mountainous seas and a howling gale, but there is nothing more than a light wind and a gentle swell. I ask what today's measurements are and I'm told force three for both wind and sea, which is light breeze and slight sea. This news doesn't make me feel any better as I'm concerned that if the ear patches aren't working at this low measurement, what will it be like if it gets rougher? I can't help but wonder if it's going to be like this for the entire journey around Antarctica.

The wind coupled with large gulps of fresh air has an instant stimulating affect. There aren't many passengers about because a lot of people are 'hibernating' in their beds. There are however, a lot of sea birds flying near the ship but I don't know enough about these birds to identify them. At this stage of the journey we've been told to look out for whales as well as sea birds. I have never seen a whale, so for me this is a very exciting prospect. I scan the sea and my hopes are raised from time to time when I notice a dark shadow lurking just under the foam of a breaking wave. A whale! No, it's just the contrasting shadow of the darker greenish-blue water of the curling wave just before it breaks. As the sea isn't yielding anything of wonder, instead I turn my attention upwards. Clouds! The sky is a blue and white kaleidoscope of ever changing patterns. There is an image of the perfect wing of a large seabird, slightly bent at the joint of the wing, the white feathers in perfect symmetry, not a blemish or a feather out of place; it is etching a flight path in the infinite blue, a transient repetition of nature in a cloud, maybe an albatross carrying the soul of someone's loved one

There's an announcement asking us to make our way to the lecture room where Geoff will be giving an educational and informative 'Introduction to Antarctica' at 10.30am. I realise how very little I know about this great continent and his talk gives us an insight into what is to come. Geoff Green is a Canadian adventurer and the leader of our expedition. He is the founder and executive director of Students on Ice, a pioneering and globally unique educational organisation, which has led to him receiving many awards including the Order of Canada, an Honorary PhD, and a Certificate of Special Congressional Recognition from the US Congress for his work with young people and the environment.

He takes students, teachers and scientists from around the world on expeditions to both the Arctic and Antarctic. I couldn't have wished for a more knowledgeable, enthusiastic and unpretentious leader as Geoff, despite all his accolades from such organisations as the Discovery Channel, World Wildlife Fund, National Audubon and the Smithsonian Institute, all of which have enlisted him to lead their groups to the world's most remote areas. I ask Geoff how his love for the polar regions started. He says:

> The real catalyst was when I got the opportunity to go to the Arctic in 1994 having previously had no experience with the Polar Regions before. I found it so powerful it turned out to be a life-changing experience which inspired and influenced my idea of taking young people to these frozen regions to give them the opportunity to experience such a life-changing journey and give the world's youth a heightened understanding and respect for our planet's global ecosystems, and inspiration to protect it. Many people thought I was mad, and it was a terrific gamble putting all my personal money into the company. What gratifies me the most is that the programme will have a lasting impact on future generations.

He was far from mad; it has grown into one of the most successful companies whose aim is conservation. Geoff is all too aware of the issues facing the polar regions and how these changes affect us all.

It is not just the youth who benefit from travelling to the polar regions—this journey is having such an impact on me, a grandmother, despite the fact that it has only just begun. I feel so lucky to have such an interesting and knowledgeable leader. And he's just one of the leaders on this expedition whose goal is to give us a heightened understanding and respect for the planet's global ecosystems.

Initially the presentation is very well attended, but one by one people start trickling out. It isn't through lack of interest, but due to the unpleasant rolling motion of the ship playing havoc with our middle ears. I try to concentrate so that my mind will be so focussed that I won't notice the game my middle ear is playing with my brain. Eventually I have to go back into the fresh air for more oxygen. Feeling seasick is the only downside of the adventure.

The Drake Passage

The infamous Drake Passage that is causing so many of us to hibernate in our cabins was named after Sir Francis Drake; he was the second European to circumnavigate the globe in 1577. Drake was secretly commissioned by Queen Elizabeth I to undertake an expedition to the Pacific coast of America to fight the Spanish. Five ships set sail from England, but by the time they reached the Pacific, only Drake's ship, the flag ship the *Pelican* remained; it was renamed the *Golden Hind*. Drake was the first Englishman to sail down the Strait of Magellan in 1578, travelling from the Atlantic in the east, to the Pacific in the west. They noticed that the land on their port side consisted of numerous islands rather than one landmass as had previously been thought. On reaching the Pacific they encountered a terrible storm which blew them South to 57 °'S. They had reached the very tip of South America—Cape Horn. To the South lay a vast stretch of sea where the waters of the Atlantic and Pacific meet. This previously unknown route became known as the Drake Passage. Its discovery meant that all European countries had access to the Pacific without having to get permission from the Spanish and Portuguese, as had previously been the case when the only known route was through the Strait of Magellan. Drake died of dysentery on 28 January 1596, just off the coast of Panama. He was buried at sea.

We are now entering an area of water where sea birds are prolific. Despite the brisk wind, if one can see through the tears blurring our vision, the deck is the best place to be. When it gets too bad the bridge provides a safe sanctuary from the Antarctic winds. I stand stock-still listening to the hauntingly shrill call of a bird arcing into infinity on the air currents. I experience a feeling of uplift deep in my soul as if it is taking me with it, high up into the feathery clouds.

Our ornithologist, Juan, tells us about the sea birds we are likely to see during our Drake Passage crossing, birds that I've never even heard of before, let alone seen. His enthusiasm and information makes every bird an individual. Juan was born and lives in Buenos Aires, but chose to go to the University of East Anglia in England to finish his education. He graduated with a BSc in biology in 2001. I ask him what, as a city dweller from birth, instigated his interest in birds. He says that his interest in wildlife began with a passion for dinosaurs at the age of six. At the age of nine his passion changed to birds and it has continued ever since. I find it amazing that he can recognise the different species of birds we see, even when they are flying some distance from the ship. Through Juan's very clear, detailed descriptions and his patience I can now tell an albatross from an antarctic fulmar – mainly because fulmars are smaller, more like the size of a gull. I can recognise a black-browed albatross if it's flying near the ship, but that's because it has prominent black eyebrows. The group of birds Juan's most passionate about is the 'tubernose' of which the albatross is a member. 'Tubernose' are sea birds that have nostrils at the top of their bills; in some species it is one long 'tube' in the centre of the bill, in others it is two, one on either side of the bill. They look like tubes, hence the name. Salt ingested when diving for fish is extracted by glands in their nostrils and expelled down the tube. Antarctica is home to six species of albatrosses.

We've just seen what is probably the most iconic sea bird in the world, the wandering albatross. It is flying very close to the ship making it easier to identify now that we have had Juan's informative talk. They are the largest sea birds in the world. Wandering 'alberts' have a wingspan up to 12 feet and weigh between 14–25 lbs. They can live for up to 85 years. Their plumage is predominantly white with black upper wings which look as if they've been dusted with snow on top. They've got large, pink bills with a curved hook on the end which resembles a sharp talon for hooking fish. They have distinctive well-defined tubernose nostrils on either side of the top of their bills. Despite their size, they are surprisingly beautiful to watch as they are arcing on the currents of air with effortless grace, as weightless and fluid as a ballerina, then suddenly dipping down and skimming the waves, their wing tips brushing the crests of foam. In complete contrast to that they look so ungainly when they land on the water and then try to get airborne again. They have to run to gain speed in order to take off as their large webbed feet thrash the water frantically as if their very lives are in danger from an underwater predator if they don't succeed. Perhaps that's why they spend so much time flying: the thought of landing in the sea and having to make such an effort to get airborne again must be very off-putting. Their breeding season lasts for up to a year, so they produce chicks in alternate years. Their courting displays are second to none; the male's vocal arias are very varied, and their seductive dancing is guaranteed to seduce the female of choice. Once the egg has hatched, it takes nine months for the chick to fledge. At the end of the breeding season the chicks are left to fend for themselves. The parent birds fly off and when they return, the chicks are still in the nest. They can fly for a distance of over 1,000 miles from their nests searching for food and remain airborne for two years without touching down. I try to imagine what my life would be like if I had to walk miles to find food, only returning home when I'd got enough to feed the family. That thought makes me appreciate the wonders of nature even more, and why our planet is so unique. The albatross was the passion of the sea bird expert, R. C. Murphy who stated, "I now belong to a higher cult of mortals, for I have seen the albatross!" When I first heard this quote I thought it was rather a strange thing to say, but following my first sighting of a wandering albatross, I feel a sense of levitation, almost as if I am flying too.

An albatross flying high above us

When I consider the vast expanse of sea we are sailing in and the fact that it is estimated that there are only about twenty thousand breeding pairs in the world, the likelihood of seeing an albatross is remote. So now I belong to that higher cult of mortals! I feel a strong belief that if I was ever shipwrecked, I'd fly to eternity on the wings of a wandering albatross along with the dead sailors in Sara Vial's beautiful poem. Now I know a little more about the incredible bird life in this remote, cold, windy part of the world, I'm excited when I see four different species of albatross during the course of the next few hours, although I find it almost impossible to tell them apart when they are at sea—I can only identify them when they come close to the ship. Juan, of course, is an expert and points out a lone grey-headed albatross, which is a beautiful bird with a glossy, black bill and very colourful bright orange and yellow stripes on the top and bottom. Now I know what to look for, a bit later on I'm able to identify a small flock of them. I feel very pleased with my progress.

What a wonderful feeling it is standing on the deck, the wind fanning my face, the smell of the sea, the taste of salt on the air, and this incredible wildlife around me.

The Antarctic Convergence

We are just entering the Antarctic Convergence, an irregular shaped boundary varying in width by 20–30 miles, it is sandwiched between two invisible boundaries: a biological border which begins at 48°S and a political border at 60°S latitude. It is where the very cold air and icy waters flowing from Antarctica collide with the warmer air and waters of the Atlantic, Pacific and Indian Oceans. The collision of these contrasting temperatures causes low pressure to build up, leading to a belt of thick fog, blizzards and a vicious storm belt known as the Antarctic Trough. Mariners refer to these adverse conditions as 'the roaring forties, furious fifties and screaming sixties'. The Antarctic Circumpolar Current, the world's largest current, flows around the Southern Ocean moving the surface water in a north easterly direction. The highly-oxygenated, icy cold northward flowing surface waters sink to the bottom of the ocean beneath the warmer waters of the sub-Antarctic islands lying north of the pack ice, reducing the temperatures of half the world's seas.

The Antarctic Convergence waters are constantly fed by strong surface currents which stir up a layer of rich nutrients and gases. There is an abundance of marine life including plants, fish and birds, making it the world's largest 'supermarket'. The Antarctic Convergence supports phytoplankton, a minute plant which blooms in abundance, trapping energy through photosynthesis and forming the basis of the food chain. It floats on the surface of the rich waters in the Antarctic summer when it is eaten by nektons, submerged sea animals such as krill and jellyfish. These sea creatures are then eaten by octopus, squid and other fish, which continue along the food chain, being eaten by penguins, seals and whales etc. and eventually by humans. It's a slap-in-the-face eye-opener to realise that if phytoplankton, an inconspicuous food source, were obliterated from the Earth's oceans, all life would eventually become extinct. If humans were wiped off the face of the earth, all other life would not only continue to survive, but would probably thrive.

When I was a child I lived in Zimbabwe (Southern Rhodesia) for two years. My father was in the Royal Air Force and was posted there. We sailed back to England on the *Sterling Castle,* a ship of the Union Castle Line. On the way back, at the age of seven, I can remember my parents telling me that we would soon be crossing 'the Line'. There was a party atmosphere on board and the ship was decorated with bunting and streamers. I stood by the railings patiently gazing into the sea, waiting to see this famous Line we were about to cross, also called the Equator. King Neptune appeared climbing over the railing of the ship having come up a ladder out of the sea, covered in seaweed and wore a gold crown. He went and sat on a throne next to his queen. I was dragged away from the ship's railing and had to go and see the 'doctor' who looked through his spectacles at me and felt my pulse, then he told me to open my mouth and say 'R'. I was then given a spoonful of a disgusting dark medicine called Coca-Cola. It was the first time I'd tasted Coke and I didn't like it—maybe it was the colour, or maybe it was because it represented medicine. To this day I have never developed a taste for it. Next, I was hustled off to meet King

Neptune, we shook hands and he gave me a certificate saying I had crossed the Line. I couldn't understand why I hadn't seen 'the Line'. My eyes had been riveted on the water, so I knew I hadn't missed it through my own negligence. I remember feeling very let down. On sports day at school, in the running race and egg and spoon race, there was a very clear line at the finishing post so you could see who'd won the race. How did people know where this line was that we had just crossed, when you couldn't see it? I suppose I was too young to understand the concepts of invisible boundaries and abstract nouns. My only consolation was that all the adults got a dunking in a big canvass bath of cold water and a bucket of water tipped over their heads—the children didn't.

Nearly sixty years on, I now understand that lines and boundaries aren't necessarily visible in concrete form, and that the line or boundary at the Equator was a geophysical area between two hemispheres, so I'm not going to stand at the ship's railing with my camera ready as we cross the Antarctic Convergence. However, the Convergence actually does have a visible line; it is formed by the oil of dead microorganisms that float on the surface and mingle with foam. It also accounts for why seabirds are so prevalent as we draw nearer the Convergence, they flock to this rich feeding ground helping to make the line more visible.

Anyway, back to the two maritime boundaries. They regulate the ecosystems of regions surrounding Antarctica. Sunlight penetrates the atmosphere and heats the Earth, but this energy is reflected back off the ice into space. There is an invisible spectrum called infrared light; this light traps carbon dioxide (CO_2) and prevents it disappearing into space, therefore keeping the planet warm. Carbon dioxide works in conjunction with water vapour rising off the oceans which is why coastal areas are warmer than further inland. It takes only a small amount of carbon dioxide to change the Earth's temperatures dramatically.

At times I feel rather unsettled as the world I know and have taken for granted all my life is suddenly taking on a new meaning and challenge. I've travelled extensively, gaining a little knowledge about other cultures, languages, religions and regions, but nothing has prepared me for such a contrast of extremes as in Antarctica. There must be hundreds of seeds that lie dormant in all of us, some of them never getting the light needed to fertilise them. A new seed in me has sprung into life. I want to know more about what is in the sky and the sea. Why is the sea and sky so blue in Antarctica? I have always associated the blueness with tropical areas although come to think of it, the sky is also a clear blue on very cold, frosty days when the sun is shining. I ask one of the leaders if he can explain it in simple language. I am told that particles in the air create far more blue light than any other colour of the spectrum and this also applies to mud particles in the oceans. I presume that's why the sky and sea are blue on a sunny day. It is light that causes the blueness, not temperature, which is why the sea and sky in Antarctica can be as blue as in the Mediterranean on a sunny day, yet Antarctica is the coldest, driest place on the planet. Young children are born with a zest for exploration and adventure; the most asked questions are "Why?" and "How?" I feel like that child, I am encountering a new world.

Into the abyss

Our Polar adventurer Belinda, tells us about life at the extreme depths of the bottom of the oceans. She is one of the world's deepest diving females and has dived to sites such as the *Titanic* and the *Bismarck*. She completed a dive to 16,000 feet in 2005. She is a certified ship's master and divemaster, and to add to these accolades, she is also a naturalist, environmental officer, logistics and safety specialist and she promotes exploration and sustainable management of the world's oceans through various education institutes. Belinda is from New Zealand and has extensive experience planning, organising and leading expeditions to far flung places around the world. All the experts on the expedition seem to go out of their way to make this a memorable journey of a lifetime. Belinda participated in the filming of the James Cameron documentary *Aliens of the Deep* (2005, and shares her knowledge and experience with us. The film shows marine life deep down in the seemingly bottomless parts of the oceans; beyond the continental shelves which were once thought to be flat, it is often referred to as the abyss. Since divers have been able to dive to such depths by descending in submersibles, they have now discovered that they contain volcanic mountains and previously unknown marine life. Plants form the basis of the food chain for all living creatures deriving their energy via photosynthesis. Cameron's *Aliens of the Deep*, takes us to incredible depths where sunlight never penetrates, so instead of the plant life producing food through photosynthesis, plants in the abyss produce food through chemosynthesis. Creatures from microscopic bacteria to larger forms of life get their food from chemicals rather than the sun. These organisms are among the oldest forms of life on our planet. James Cameron thought it was similar to visiting another planet inhabited by unfamiliar creatures. Exploration and filming would not have been possible without present day submersibles. Watching this film has opened up a new part of the natural world that I would never normally get the chance to see. I'm sure the images of the quite grotesque marine life, which looks like something from a science fiction thriller, will leave an indelible imprint on my memory. I honestly feel as if I'm diving deep down into an incredible new universe, but without feeling scared or claustrophobic.

The water around Antarctica is so cold it would kill most living things, yet sea animals and plants thrive in water below zero degrees. The water itself doesn't freeze because of the salt content, but strangely nor do the sea creatures that inhabit this inhospitable environment. They have their own antifreeze in their blood, tissues and bodies which they make out of protein. If they couldn't do this, ice crystals would form in their tissues ripping them apart. Antarctic waters contain twice as much oxygen as tropical waters. Sea spiders in Antarctica can be 3000 times bigger than in European waters, they have a lower metabolic rate than animals elsewhere. The ice has kept temperatures low and constant for at least 25 million years, making Antarctica a more constant environment than anywhere else on Earth. This constant temperature enables animals and plants time to adapt and thrive.

Belinda also shows us a film of the submersible diving she does, including to the RMS *Titanic*. I think I would find it very scary to go down to such depths and see the ghostly, inert body of the *Titanic*. It seems very eerie watching it on the screen. Unlike the James Cameron film, my feelings of unease are as much to do with the catastrophe that befell the *Titanic* as it is claustrophobic fear I have of deep water and the dark. *Aliens of the Deep* tells a very positive story about the tenacity and endurance of the thriving life in the natural world deep in the ocean. *Titanic* tells the horrific, but true story of the loss of human life in very contrasting conditions. From the sophisticated shipboard life of a luxury liner on its maiden voyage, gliding across the top of the ocean waves; an evening of fun and merriment, to the horror of it all coming to a sudden halt; for many ending their life's journey in icy depths and oblivion.

After Belinda's informative tales of the amazing life in the 'underworld', I feel compelled to go up on deck and gaze in wonder at what lies below the water we are travelling across. How different things seem after absorbing all that information compared to my previous view that water was the same the world over, just changing in temperature, colour and the size of the waves. Even the fresh air seems different as the cold wind whips up the waves. I wish I could make my own antifreeze! The bracing air must be having a beneficial effect as at least I'm managing to stay upright with my eyes open. However I'm very aware that there is another day of this to come before we reach Antarctica.

Every evening a schedule for the following day's programme is put through our cabin door. It begins with a brief recap on what we did the day before, then provides the itinerary for the following day. It's only a guideline as the weather conditions have the ultimate say.

The daylight hours are packed full of interesting stories and information, the evening is a time for reflection and a drink or two in the bar with like-minded people. At night I'm beginning to enjoy sliding up and down in my bed, listening to the ship's creaking lullaby. Tomorrow we should see Antarctica.

4. OUR FIRST LANDING

There is an announcement that a pod of fin whales has been spotted on the starboard side so Captain Kiselev very kindly slows the ship down so that we can get a better view. Seasickness forgotten, everyone rushes to the railings with cameras clicking. Blue whales are the largest in the world, fin whales are the second largest, up to 89 feet in length and weighing up to 130 tons.

The feelings I'm experiencing are as churned up as the foaming sea. I'm wildly excited and bursting with energy, yet at the same time I'm mesmerised and calm. They are the first whales I've ever seen. They are such awe-inspiring marine creatures, they look as large as a submarine furtively lurking below the water and then suddenly surfacing for a short time before submerging again. The females are slightly longer than the males but it's hard to distinguish which is male or female as it's impossible to see the entire length of their bodies above the waterline. They have elongated bodies and narrow V-shaped heads which make them look like large torpedoes. The left side of their jaw is black, but the right side is white. The dorsal fins are very prominent and their bellies and back are grooved and ridged. Ingrid, our marine biologist, tells us that instead of teeth they have baleen, which are about two feet long with 300–400 horny fringed plates on either side. She explains that these act like a sieve, filtering water and trapping small sea creatures that they feed on. To breathe, they have to come to the surface to inhale and exhale; this is called blowing, which they repeat five to eight times a minute before submerging for between four and twenty minutes. The blow is not water that they have swallowed as I used to think, it's vapour from their lungs just like a human exhaling, but we can't see vapour in human breath unless it's very cold. They live for about 80 years, travel in pods and give birth to one calf every two to three years, which

47

weighs two tons and is about 20 feet long. (And you thought your long labour was due to having a large baby!)

Apart from the whales, we are rewarded with the sight of another wandering albatross and there are cape petrels which are following the ship scavenging for food. They are quite easy to identify, with a distinctive white underside on their bodies and wings, dark, chequered upper body and wings, and a black head. They nest on cliffs so never stray too far from land.

The tannoy system crackles into life and Geoff announces that we will be making our first landing some time after lunch—a thrill of excitement like an electrical current passes through me. We have to drag ourselves away from the deck and go to the lecture room for a Zodiac safety briefing and visitor guidelines. Rigid inflatable boats (RIBs), or Zodiacs as we know them, will take us from the ship to the shore. This involves going down a wooden gangplank on one side of the ship, then stepping into the Zodiac. We are told we must not jump but step in carefully. I am soon to find out that this is easier said than done when there's a swell, making the gangplank and Zodiacs at odds with gravity. There is always a member of the team to drive the Zodiac, and one to help us on and off. We are told we must grip round the wrist not the hand as we step from the ladder to the Zodiac because you get a firmer grip round the wrist. Life jackets are hanging on hooks on our cabin doors which we have to put on before entering the Zodiacs. We are told to take nothing away from the land, not even a pebble or a feather, but take only our photos and memories. We must leave nothing behind on the land except our footprints and, most importantly, we must not let any plastic bags protecting our camera equipment blow away. We will hear about the serious consequence of the devastating effects plastic bags can have later.

Once dressed in all our waterproof clothing and life jackets, and before leaving the ship, we have to go to what's called the mud-room. There is a list of names with a number besides each one and mine is 21. Next to that is a board with bright yellow numbered tags. We have to flip our tags over before disembarking and flip them back again once back on board. This is so that the leaders know who has left the ship, and at the end of the excursion they can check that nobody has been left behind on land.

A Zodiac in action, still coated with ice

We also have to walk through a disinfectant tray and scrub our boots before we disembark, and then repeat the procedure when we come back on board.

What a relief to see for ourselves that at long last we aren't far from the 'Unique White Continent'. After lunch I go back on deck to see our first iceberg floating past. It's like an ice sculpture of weird shape, mainly glistening white in colour, but streaked with iridescent blue. We are told it is a 'growler', which is a small iceberg that has rolled over, originally having calved off from a glacier, or the melting remains of a tabular iceberg that broke away from the ice-shelf many years ago. It gets its name from the sound it makes when it rolls over, a bit like a creaking door.

There is great excitement as we glimpse our first sight of land, not far south of the Antarctic Convergence. The first thing we see is a ghostly, sheer, dark cliff that looks like a fortress in the middle of the ocean. Behind it, in stark contrast, there are further gently undulating cliffs covered in thick white snow. Pyramid-shaped cliffs appear from nowhere, like cones randomly scattered in the sea, then suddenly a dark form that resembles Cape Town's Table Mountain with a cloth of white snow looms up in the distance. This is followed by pinnacles of rock standing like sentries guard-

49

ing the entrance of the bay that we are heading for. As we draw nearer, there are more and more weird and wonderful shapes mushrooming out of the grey sea. Some are like fairy tale castles with delicate pointed turrets and minarets; some have a stark naked beauty about them unlike anything I've ever seen before. Very occasionally the sun peeps out from behind the clouds floating by on the breath of the atmosphere; destination unknown. Our spirits are high with a buzz of excitement. We are in Antarctica! The Drake Passage and Antarctic Convergence crossing has been worth it.

At last the ship drops anchor not far from Aitcho Island (HO Island) which is where we are going to set foot on Antarctica for the first time. It is one of the islands in the South Shetland archipelago, situated at 61° 50'S. The name actually comes from the Hydrographic Office of the UK Admiralty. Hydrography is the description, measurement and charting of the Earth's seas, oceans, lakes and rivers; it also includes tides, currents and waves. This research is very important for navigational purposes as well as understanding the world's life giving water systems.

Everyone is up and about, even those who had succumbed to the dreaded seasickness. We all duly disinfect our boots and form a queue along the deck by the ladder. Before anyone is allowed off the ship Belinda, our deep sea diver, shouts out "Have you all flipped your tags?" In the excitement a number of us, including me, have forgotten. We all troop back inside to flip them. That means going through the disinfecting ritual again. A bit of a pain, but better than introducing diseases onto the land. It's our responsibility to remember after all!

There are five Zodiacs; each carries a maximum of 10 people with only two at a time allowed on the ladder. Although the sea looks calm, there is quite a swell alongside the ship. I get the wrist hold right, but lose my balance and jump into the Zodiac. I'm not very big, but I can see why it's dangerous to jump as it makes the boat rock. Trust me to rock the boat! We zoom towards land, skimming the tops of the waves. The wind has dropped so my first experience of riding in a Zodiac is exhilarating and I thoroughly enjoy it. We are soon on the edge of the surf and come to rest on the black volcanic sandy beach, flanked by spectacular dark cliffs to one side, and low hills of differing gradients on the other side. They stretch as far as the eye can see; most of them covered with snow and penguins. There are safety rules regarding getting in and out of the Zodiacs on the shoreline. We have to sit at the front facing away from the beach, swing one leg over the side so we are straddling it, and then swing the other leg over and stand up on the edge of the surf.

On landing the first thing that hits me is the terrible stench of guano (penguin poo); an acrid cocktail of rotting fish and seaweed, so overpowering it makes me feel quite sick. Fortunately it doesn't take long for my olfactory senses to become accustomed to it. We are greeted by a group of gentoo penguins. They are smaller than I imagined, weighing around 12 lbs and are 27.5 inches tall. They appear to be very fashion conscious with colour coordinated feet and bills in a very attractive coral colour. They have rather overdone the 'eyeshadow', a thick white stripe above the eyes which looks as if they have been experimenting with make-up for the first time. They are strongly bound to their mate, often staying together throughout the year, unlike most species which only come together at the breeding season. They don't stick to the same breeding site each year so they are not territorial. If they lose an egg or a chick, they quickly lay a second clutch of eggs. This year's chicks are nearly adult and moulting, making them look scruffy with their sleek, black adult plumage suddenly broken by grey, fluffy patches of down. They are as numerous as pebbles on the beach.

We've been told not to go up to the penguins, but let them come to us. They are very friendly; one waddles up to me and stands within touching distance looking up at me as if he/she wants to engage in deep and meaningful conversation. I'm mesmerised and kneel on the wet sand to take a photo. Not wanting to be left out of the picture another waddles up and puts his face close to the lens. It's amazing how friendly and fearless they are. They remind me of chubby, inquisitive toddlers; they have that same innocent trust that is so appealing, making me want to protect them from harm. Their vulnerability tugs at my heartstrings. Some of them come up and are pecking at my trouser legs. I can't believe how tame they are. How different from the Magellanic penguins I'd seen in Tierra del Fuego; they were terrified of humans and disappeared underground into their nests, or dived straight back into the water when I came near them. I had expected the gentoo penguins to run as far away from us as possible, meaning we'd have to view them from a distance. I think they know we are their friends as we frighten the skuas away.

There is a constant take off and landing of brown skuas. They strut around aggressively, terrifying the penguins and me too at times. They eat penguin eggs and baby chicks. They are large brown gull-like birds weighing up to 6lbs and have a wingspan of up to five feet three inches. They often nest very near penguin rookeries so they have a ready stocked larder within pecking distance. They return to the same partner and breeding ground every year and defend their territory against other skuas. They are very aggressive and sometimes dive bomb humans. I suppose they see us as a threat to their food supply. It is thought that some migrate as far north as the Arctic during the austral (southern hemisphere's) winter.

I was once dive bombed by a large bird (not a skua) while I was walking round the ruins of a Jesuit Mission in Argentina. I was really frightened and couldn't understand why it had picked on me to attack. Then I stopped dead in my tracks as I nearly trod on a nest full of eggs on the ground. The poor bird was trying to protect its soon-to-be-hatched babies. Antarctic skuas dive bomb humans because we are a threat to their food supply, or rather our presence prevents them from getting to the food; there is no way any of us would want to tuck into penguin eggs or baby chicks for dinner.

I can see a smaller group of chinstrap penguins standing together a bit further along the beach. Chinstraps weigh 10 lbs and have an average height of 27 inches. They breed only north of the Antarctic Circle and are abundant in the South Shetland Islands. They are usually found in ice-free waters as they feed on krill. They are called chinstrap because they have a very distinctive black stripe under their chins that looks like the strap of a helmet. This makes them very easy to identify. They return to the same breeding ground every year, preferring rocky, steep, boulder-covered ground. They mate with the same partner each year;

providing they each survive another year. They are territorial and can become quite aggressive to the point of driving away any other penguins that have got there first. The chinstrap penguins mostly ignore us, but some come up close to give us the once-over. The gentoo and chinstrap don't seem to mix together, preferring to stay within their own groups.

Penguins have more feathers than any other species of bird. When explorers first came to Antarctica and saw these flightless birds, they thought that they had evolved from dinosaurs and that their feathers had once been dinosaur scales. It was thought that they must be the most primitive bird species in the world. In 1911 three men from Scott's Terra Nova Expedition set out to try and verify this theory. They were Henry Bowers, Apsley Cherry-Garrard and Edward Wilson. They wanted to collect eggs from emperor penguins which entailed a 57-mile journey inland to Cape Crozier. This had to be undertaken in the middle of winter, the breeding time for emperor penguins, in temperatures of -61° C. Having collected a number of eggs which they carried back in their mittens, some of the eggs got broken as they stumbled and fell over the rough, icy terrain. They managed to save three eggs which were to be sent back to England for scientific study. It was thought that by analysing the embryos they could find a link back to dinosaurs. The primitive theory was rejected—scientists discovered that there was no similarity to the prehistoric creatures. They actually proved to be the most recent bird species on the planet along with tubernose such as the albatross. One of the three remaining eggs brought back to England is on display at the Natural History Museum in London.

The sky is silvery-grey, but not heavy. The sun is almost visible as if it's hiding behind a gauze curtain like a dim light bulb on a stage set. We are free to walk around, but to start with we all stay on the black, volcanic, sandy beach where we've landed. There's so much to take in and keep us absorbed in the way of wildlife and scenery that it's hard for the eyes and senses to adjust to it all. We are content to stay on this part of the island where we've landed for the time being. Apart from the penguins there are a lot of different kinds of seaweed. The predominant kind is a dark red species that seems to be a favourite in the penguins' diet as they peck at it with relish. I presume it's this unappetising mixture of fish and seaweed that makes their guano smell so overpowering

A bit later most of us go for a walk over a low hill. It is good to be on terra firma again. Cushion moss is growing on the island; I hadn't expected to see any plant life in this inhospitable climate. We see antarctic fur seals and elephant seals. The elephant seals don't have the same mesmerising affect on me as the penguins have. They look rather like gigantic slugs with flippers. I'm not particularly impressed … that is until I'm given some very interesting information about them. Their Latin name is (*Mirounga leonine*) known as true seals (*Phocidae*) of which there are nineteen species. The fur seals are eared seals with the Latin name (*Arctocephalus gazella*) of which there are fifteen species (*Otariidae*). The difference is that *Otariidae* have ears and *Phocidae* don't. In some species the ears are very prominent, sticking out on either side of their heads, they look a bit like very small handlebars. In others they have only an oval hole of no more than one centimetre which closes under water. They have acute hearing when underwater and can detect the direction of sounds. On land their hearing is about the same as that of humans. Evidence suggests they use sonar to find food, navigate and to avoid predators and obstacles; they often hunt faster in total darkness. Their whiskers provide radar and act like very sensitive antennae that can feel underwater vibrations from even very small fish. They have an average of 40 whiskers on either side, which can be up to 20 inches long. They close their nostrils completely when under water, but must come up to breathe every 30 minutes for adults, about half that for youngsters. Usually on land, their pupils are no more than vertical slits, but under water they dilate and light is amplified through a special layer behind the retina. They have upper and lower eyelids which protect their eyes, but they also have a third lid called a nictitating membrane, an inner eyelid, which acts like a windscreen wiper to remove sand.

Most seals use their front flippers to haul themselves around on land. The back flippers are not used on land because they can't rotate them forwards, they're webbed and turned backwards so they are used like a rudder to propel them through the water. The exception to this are fur seals, who are able to rotate them so both

Southern elephant seals

front and back flippers are used to walk around on land in a very awkward, ungainly fashion, but they keep them tucked in close to their bodies when swimming. Their main diet is fish and krill, but strangely they also eat stones—up to 24 lbs of small stones have been found in their stomachs. It's thought they are probably used for grinding up food, or to crush parasitic worms.

Their flippers fascinate me and get me thinking about evolution. When my daughter-in-law, Justine, was five weeks pregnant with James, at her first check-up she was told that the baby now had ears and flippers. Because we didn't know the gender of the child I always referred to it as flipper. Strangely enough when he was about eight months old and starting to move around, he used to drag himself across the floor on his tummy using his arms like flippers to pull himself along. He was obviously not a fur seal as his back flippers, I mean legs and feet, didn't play any part in his movement across the floor. In the swimming pool his legs and feet moved with the agility of any seal's flippers. I was quite disappointed when he underwent metamorphoses about a month later and started crawling. I could put myself in Darwin's shoes as I'd discovered the similarities between a human baby and an aquatic mammal. Did we evolve from the sea? Our tears are salty, our blood is salty and our sweat is salty. Is our amniotic fluid salty? It's not really a thing anyone would want to taste. I believe foetuses in the womb swallow copious amounts of it, but we never remember. It's not really a thing I've given any thought to before, but somehow watching these seals and their life in salty water suddenly makes me wonder. After a quick search I learn that about 98 per cent of the amniotic fluid is water, and 2 per cent salt.

Learning more about these marine animals has completely changed my perception of them. Almost like watching the transformation of the story of Cinderella, from rags to riches; I now see them in a different light and they begin to enchant me. I make eye contact with a female lolling in the sand, the expression in her eyes says so much. The light is very hazy so her pupils are quite well dilated and sad looking. They say that the eyes are the mirror of the soul and I'm sure she's trying to talk to me with her eyes. Maybe I look sad too as I remember reading a book about the slaughter of baby seals entitled *Savage Luxury* by Brian Davis. The author describes the barbarity of commercial sealing in the past when hunters clubbed baby seals on the head and skinned them alive while they were still conscious. The mother had to witness the painful slaughter of her baby and was powerless to stop the hunter. Davis wrote: "I saw the heart in a body without skin, beating frantically. After the hunter had left the ice, I saw the mother seal crawl back to the shattered carcass of her pup. Great tears flowed from her eyes". Why all this suffering for greed, fashion and outward show in the form of sealskin coats? I don't need to say any more. I wish I could apologise to the cow seal for the inhumanity of some of my species and tell her that we won't harm her. I believe that book brought about drastic changes in seal hunting. Reluctantly I have to leave the trusting looking seals with their beguiling, big, sad eyes, and move on.

The view on the other side of the hill presents a picture that literally stops us in our tracks. Two bays merge together; their waters coming from opposite directions, meeting like old friends stopping for a chat. Standing guard in the middle is a rock pinnacle of an extraordinary shape, it stands tall like a lighthouse; it has an oval shaped 'body' and a pinnacle that reaches skyward

The rock pinnacle on Aitcho Island—in the foreground a multitude of penguins.

like the tower of a cathedral with a spire on the top. On the left side the hill is higher with a dusting of snow, and beyond that there is a large, dark basalt rock, not unlike a tabular iceberg in shape. Behind that there are ghostly-white mountains covered with thick snow. On the other side there are dark, brooding cliffs rising from the volcanic sand. I can't believe how the terrain can be so different in such a small area. It reminds me of a description of sandcastles that my friend Daphne described to me following a visit to Vietnam. She said that children make them by getting handfuls of wet sand which they drizzle through their fingers to form rugged pinnacle shapes. In England children build sandcastles by filling buckets with sand and tipping them over to make smooth, round or square turrets. How much are we unconsciously influenced by the topography of the land we see? The terrain in Vietnam must be far more rugged than the smoother, more rounded hills of England.

There are gigantic whale bones littering the beach. They are mainly large ribs and vertebrae. The holes in the vertebrae are the size of the seat of a stool and filled with snow. The bones that stick out on the sides are the size of cricket bats. I take a photo of one that looks just like a plane that is about to take off, or that has just landed. Its nose is the hole stuffed with snow, the vertebrae projections on either side are like wings, and the upright bone is the tail. Amid this rather surreal 'painting' there are a few gentoo penguins, many of which have almost fully grown chicks that are still being fed by their mothers with what looks like a disgusting fish soup. They are completely unconcerned by our invasion of their territory. There are also a few chinstrap penguins which are just standing around either enjoying the view, or waiting to take off out to sea as winter approaches. The marine animals and birds in Antarctica are amazing. It is almost as if there was a mass immigration of wildlife to a promised land where they would be safe from human interference.

Time passes all too quickly amidst this landscape and reluctantly we zoom back to the ship on the Zodiacs. About 10 minutes after the last passenger has re-embarked, there is another call from Belinda: "Have you all flipped your tags back? If not, we've left a number of people on the island." Once again I'm one of them.

I admire her patience. I suppose the awe-inspiring experience we've just had is blocking mundane thoughts such as flipping a tag. I think I'm up in the clouds somewhere.

A true adventurer

Back on board everyone has got their sea legs, and a healthy appetite. I sit next to 83-year-old Norman Baker, a man with a zest for life and very interesting stories to relate. He tells me about the building and testing of reed boats to discover if it was possible for Mediterranean civilisations to cross the Atlantic to America 4,000 years ago. Thor Heyerdahl, the Norwegian ethnographer and adventurer, famous for his *Kon-Tiki* expedition, engaged Norman as navigator, radioman and second-in-command on his three reed boat expeditions on boats called *Ra*, *Ra 11* and *Tigris*. They wanted to prove that ancient seafarers travelled much further than previously expected. They constructed the boats from reeds called tortora, then sailed from Morocco to Barbados in 1970 and proved it was possible to cross great seas in such a boat. I shiver at the thought of making such a crossing. Thank goodness for ships like the *Akademik Shokalskiy*. Norman also served on a destroyer engaged in troop support and shore bombardment during the Korean War in 1950–3.

Norman later married a lady named Mary Anne and during their honeymoon in Switzerland, he realised his childhood dream of climbing the Matterhorn. Was that the end of Norman's adventures? No, they didn't stop there! His wife and children were avid participants in his adventurous life. While he was working as an engineer, Norman was also the captain of the sailing schooner *Anne Kristine*. It was a Norwegian ship that was built in 1868 and was one of the oldest vessels plying the open seas, carrying out ocean research. The ship needed quite a lot of work doing to her, so Norman and his wife and children set about rebuilding her when they were in the British Virgin Islands, making her ready to sail in the Tall Ships Parade for the Statue of Liberty Centennial Celebration in New York. Most recently he participated in research expeditions to Easter Island (Rapa Nui) 3,878 km off the coast of Chile in the South Pacific. Though sadly now widowed he continues his adventurous life, his fearlessness (becoming that evening) an inspiration for me to take forward in the future—a truly remarkable man. Both on- and off-shore it has been a very interesting and memorable day and I am left wondering what tomorrow will hold.

5. ANTARCTIC FIRE AND ICE
In the footsteps of Captain Cook

In 1772–5 Captain James Cook became the first man to circum-navigate the Antarctic continent in command of HMS *Resolution* and HMS *Adventure.* Sailing to latitudes never before explored. On 17 January 1773 he became the first to cross the Antarctic Circle at 71°'S, but he didn't get close enough to the land to see anything beyond ice. He thought it was a place that was not worth bothering with as it was nothing but an empty wilderness of ice; there was no certainty that land actually existed. Cook's adventurous journey inspired people from many nations to follow in his wake. Some went on scientific voyages of discovery, while others went for commercial whaling and sealing purposes. In 1820 the Russian sailor, Admiral Thaddeus von Bellingshausen sailed to Antarctica and was the first to see land; proving *tierra incognita* actually did exist.

Following on from Captain Cook's sea-faring expedition to Antarctica and Bellinghausen's sighting of land, Captain James Clark Ross was dispatched to Antarctica by the Royal Navy to study terrestrial magnetism and locate the Magnetic South Pole; he had already discovered the Magnetic North Pole in 1831. He and his men sailed in two ships, *Erebus* and *Terror* and on New Year's Day 1841, Ross and his men crossed the Antarctic Circle and entered what is now called the Ross Sea. They got close enough to the land to be able to see a massive range of mountains which they named the Admiralty Range. Their hoped-for landing was blocked by mountainous cliffs of ice, some as high as 10,000 feet.

Fire and brimstone in Antarctica is at its most ferocious on land bordering the Ross Sea and Ross and his team encountered an active volcano rising to 12,520 feet. The surgeon on *Erebus*,

Robert McCormick, described it as, 'A stupendous volcanic mountain in high state of activity.' It was named Mount Erebus after one of the ships. Scientists were later to conclude that Erebus is more than a million years old and is the most active volcano in Antarctica—it is in fact, continuously active and is part of the Pacific Ring of Fire. The crater is a glowing lava lake of fire, a bubbling red hot 'stew' from the bowels of the earth which explodes throwing up volcanic bombs in all directions. Sulphurous fumes of smoke curl into the sky above it. There is a smaller, extinct volcano next to Mt Erebus which Ross and his crew named Mt Terror after the other ship.

They encountered Antarctic pack-ice: sea that has frozen over, broken into pieces and drifted into concentrated areas. The *Erebus* and *Terror* had been strengthened to withstand ice and they were able to make a passage through into the open sea, but they couldn't penetrate through the Great Ice Barrier that hugs the actual landmass where they'd hoped to land. An ice barrier is the outer edge of sea ice that has attached itself to land; it can be several miles thick. Even if landing had been possible their quest for the magnetic South Pole would have been thwarted by a range of mountains rising to 8,000 feet. Like Captain Cook, they didn't manage to actually set foot on the continent.

It is in the path of these famous explorers that we are now heading and hoping for better luck. We get our first sight of the mainland of the continent as we sail down Antarctic Sound where the contrast of extremes is certainly making its presence felt. Precipitous mountain cliffs of brooding, basalt rock soar into the sky, dwarfing everything around; they are interspersed with rugged blue and white glaciers. An incredible 98 per cent of the Antarctic landmass is covered by an ice sheet, a thick layer of permanent ice up to two and a half miles thick, elevating the continent to over 8,000 feet, and covering an area of more than 20,000 miles wide. It originally fell as snow that became compressed into ice by the weight and it continues to be fed by annual snowfall. It is the largest sheet of ice on Earth. Dark peaks suddenly appear above the ice which look like the head of a seal popping up out of an ice hole. The snow on these peaks is called an ice cap, layers of snow that has fallen over millennia, usually on the highest point where it clings tenaciously to the rock. In the valleys between the mountains the compressed snow forms glaciers which very gradually slide down to the coastal area of the continental shelf. It is hard to imagine that below these giant rivers of ice there is red hot fire just waiting to leap up like a jack-in-the-box when the whim takes it.

We get our first sight of the mainland of the continent as we sail down Antarctic Sound; the water is calm as a millpond by comparison to what has gone before. The Sound is between seven and twelve miles wide and thirty miles long. It is also known as 'Iceberg Alley'. The reason for this nickname soon becomes obvious; it is where most of the tabular icebergs end up when massive chunks of ice break off the ice shelves on the north eastern side of Antarctica. An ice shelf is a thick, permanently floating slab of ice which forms when glaciers and the ice sheet flow down to the coastline where it freezes instantly because it is pure, fresh water. The thickness varies from 100 to 1,000 metres. It meets the icy sea growing larger as more ice flows behind it. This combined union of ice covers a huge area making Antarctica the fifth largest continent. Ice shelves can survive for thousands of years. Many of these ice shelves have been breaking up rapidly in recent years; the changing temperatures and currents can cause it to break off at its weakest points. When this happens, the resulting gigantic slabs of ice are known as tabular icebergs.

> *And then there came both mist and snow,*
> *And it grew wondrous cold:*
> *And ice mast high came flotating by*
> *As green as emerald*
> (Samuel Taylor Coleridge, *The Rime of the Ancient Mariner*)

I go up on deck and see the most amazing icebergs imaginable. I thought the growlers I'd seen were spectacular, but even larger ones appear as if from nowhere. They are ice sculptures of weird and wonderful shapes that glow with blue light in the gleaming, jagged white ice; they are surely from another planet. Suddenly, looming up on the starboard side, the giant of all icebergs appears on the horizon. Watching a tabular iceberg looming up in the distance, getting bigger and bigger until it towers above the ship, is an awe-inspiring experience. There are no words to describe it, but the memory of seeing my first one and the feeling of awe will remain with me forever. They can measure more than 60 miles long and 60 miles wide, and rise to a height of 100 feet above the waterline. This height accounts for a mere 10 per cent, meaning that a massive 90 per cent is below the waterline.

It has suddenly occurred to me that a tabular iceberg is roughly the same size as my whole county of Hampshire. It gives me an image to compare it with, perspective is so hard to see in such a massive body of water as the Southern Ocean. Tabular icebergs are thousands of years old; they are the grandfathers of the ice, unlike the newly formed sea ice which often cracks, making ice islands that float away on the ocean currents like disobedient children running away from their wise old grandparent. They are the largest in the world and are only found in the Southern Ocean. They are driven by ocean currents, but rarely cause a problem to shipping as they show up clearly on ships' radar. If they do get stranded in a shipping lane, they are very difficult to move and can take several days just to move them a few feet. If the sea temperatures rise just a little, this will melt the ice below the water line.

Having watched Belinda's dive to the *Titanic*, a ship forty times the size of the *Shokalskiy*, I'm a little concerned that we might hit a tabular iceberg. My fears are quite unnecessary as we are travelling a hundred years after the sinking of the *Titanic* and navigation and radar have moved on since then. The navigation officer completely puts my mind at rest when he tells me about how bergs are monitored.

When the sea ice breaks off, it floats on the currents and the resulting tabular icebergs are tracked and named by the US National Oceans Office when they meet three basic rules: 1) An iceberg must measure at least 10 nautical miles along its largest axis 2) A sighting must have occurred within the last 30 days; this does not apply if it is grounded or locked in fast ice so it cannot move 3) It will be tracked only as long as it remains south of 60° 'S. An archive of all icebergs tracked by the National Ice Centre has been kept since 1976. Every iceberg has its point of origin documented and is given a number and name, this enables scientists to monitor the size, what part of Antarctica it originated in, and where the ocean currents are taking it. This can tell a lot about climate change when bergs are monitored over a period of time. If all the ice in Antarctica melted, sea levels would to rise by 198 feet (60 metres) worldwide which would have a disastrous effect on the planet.

We continue our journey along 'Iceberg Alley' looking out for whales, gazing in wonder at the gigantic, artistically sculptured icebergs, and watching the dramatic scenery of the Tabarin Peninsula on the mainland of the Antarctic continent. We are heading towards Erebus and Terror Gulf on the north-eastern tip of the Antarctic Peninsula, aiming to land on historic Paulet Island, but we've been warned of bad weather ahead. Terror Gulf is hardly a name to inspire confidence; rather more to give one an overwhelming sense of trepidation. However, we are not on a luxury cruise ship, but are intrepid explorers with a lust for adventure, so the name also holds that magic of the unexpected.

Paulet Island is a small, circular volcanic island, now extinct, rising to a height of 1,158 feet. It is home to a large colony of penguins and seals, a home that is only one and a half kilometres in diameter. Its human history dates back to 1901 when a Swedish expedition led by Otto Nordenskjöld, a professor of geology and chemistry, sailed to Antarctica on the ship *Antarctic* to carry out meteorological and magnetic surveys. The *Antarctic* was under the command of Captain Carl Larsen. On reaching the north eastern tip of the Antarctic Peninsula, Larsen dropped Nordenskjold and five of his men off on Snow Hill Island where they set up a winter camp; they were the first people to overwinter in Antarctica. Captain Carl Larsen arranged to come back and pick them up the following spring. As prearranged, Larsen went back to pick up Nordenskjöld and his men, but before reaching them, disaster struck; the ship became stuck in ice about 25 miles from Snow Hill Island and a sledging party of three men set off to try and reach Nordenskjöld and his men and bring them back to the ship. The three men were unable to reach Snow Hill Island which meant Nordenskjöld's party were forced to spend a second winter marooned on the island. The three men who had gone to rescue them were also marooned. Not long after their departure the ship began to sink; there was just time to gather together a few necessary belongings before Larsen gave the order to abandon ship. The men watched as the *Antarctic* slowly sank lower and lower, finally being swallowed up by the ice as it drifted to the bottom of the seabed. It took two weeks for Larsen and his team of six men to walk across the ice to Paulet Island, where they painstakingly gathered stones to build a hut. They knew the long Antarctic winter was all they had to look forward to until the following spring when they hoped to be rescued. They survived physically by eating penguin and seal meat, and psychologically by dreaming of being rescued. Five of the men lived to tell the tale leaving behind one solitary grave on the island. Incredibly, after two winters marooned in ice, the three parties met up purely by chance and were rescued and returned home. The ruins of the hut still remain on the beach and are an attraction for visitors to explore and get a feel for what life must have been like for the men. Antarctic Sound is named after the ship *Antarctic*. Unfortunately our landing on Paulet Island isn't possible due to bad weather, so we continue on down Iceberg Alley in the hope that the weather will improve.

Call My Bluff

As always plans are dependent on the weather and sea conditions. After lunch we are told that we are going to try and make a landing at Brown Bluff which is located on the tip of the Antarctic Peninsula. It is a flat-topped volcano which erupted through a glacial lake. To me it looks similar in shape to Ayers Rock in Australia. Unlike Ayers Rock, it is covered in snow and surrounded by icebergs.

We all wait eagerly for the Brown Bluff announcement. It will be our first landing on the mainland of the Antarctic continent. The tannoy crackles into life and in excited anticipation we listen to the announcement. Not good news. Our hoped for landing is put on hold for a while; in true Antarctic style we are suddenly engulfed in a swirling blizzard of driving snow with winds gusting in excess of 50 knots. It's a complete white-out; I feel as if I'm locked in a freezing cocoon and there's no way out of it. It's

The view from the bridge during a blizzard

impossible to see anything through the windows on the bridge as they are covered by a curtain of thick snow and ice. I hope the crew know where they're going without being able to see through the navigation window. It has a sign on it which says, 'NAVIGA-TION WINDOW STAND CLEAR'. We all stand clear, but the snow ignores the command and clings to the window like a coat of thick, white paint, completely obliterating everything. Antarctic blizzards are caused by freezing cold air rushing down from the Pole where it meets the warmer air from the coast. It could have waited until we'd landed and returned to the ship!

As Admiral Richard Byrd said in his book, *Alone*, "There is something extravagantly insensate about an Antarctic blizzard at night. Its vindictiveness cannot be measured on an anemometer sheet. It is more than just wind: it is a solid wall of snow moving at gale force, pounding like surf. The whole malevolent rush is concentrated upon you as upon a personal enemy."

Explorers don't give up easily. The blizzard's game is short lived and as if laughing at us, it twirls off to cause havoc elsewhere. Geoff and two other leaders, Shane and Ingrid, decide to test the water. They go on the foredeck, brush some of the snow off one of the Zodiacs, and lower it into the freezing waters. They set off towards Brown Bluff only to return with the news that landing is impossible due to the stiff wind and brash ice near the shore.

Shane and Ingrid about to test the water. Sadly a visit to Brown Bluff was not to be.

Brash ice is small blocks of melted sea or glacier ice that look like slabs of white stone, they are blown by the wind and ocean currents causing them to completely block access to the land. Some of us brave the stinging snow on our faces to welcome Geoff and the others back. Just another typical day-to-day hazard in Antarctica! It makes me feel that we are no more than play things in the forces of nature. Many of us go back onto the slippery deck for more icebergs and whale watching and even more photos.

We enter Hope Bay at the northern tip of the Antarctic Peninsula, passing the Argentinean research base of Esperanza (which means hope in Spanish). It was formerly a British base which was built in 1975. It is a working scientific base and is unlike any other in Antarctica as the first human birth in Antarctica was recorded here. There is a school, a post office, a mayor and military detachment. Generators provide electricity. Not an easy paradise to live in, but it gives the Argentineans a right to claim sovereignty. Their motto is 'Permanence, an act of sacrifice'. World sea levels are monitored in Hope Bay, and other scientific research carried out here includes seismology, geology, glaciology and coastal ecology. We sail back towards the Bransfield Strait and head south along the Tabarin Peninsula.

6. DECEPTION: HELL'S GATE

"I felt as though I had been plumped upon another planet
or into another geologic horizon of which man had no
knowledge or memory."
Admiral Richard E Byrd, *Alone*.

Travelling south west we are sailing over a chain of inactive volcanoes on the ocean floor. They rise to a height of about 500 metres which is well below the surface of the water—they are known as seamounts. We are heading to an active volcano and the enticing crater of water at Deception Island, inviting the resident wildlife and visitors alike to take the plunge.

I've had a peaceful night's sleep and wake up at 6am I take advantage of the early bird breakfast of coffee and croissants. As dawn is breaking we head towards Bailey Head on the outer wall of Deception Island, where we hope to make an early morning landing, unfortunately the swell is making this impossible. Just beyond Bailey Head we pass a group of very sharp, vertical, black rock formations that look like giant needles rising out of the sea. Not wanting to miss anything I go up on deck. We've now arrived at 62° 59'S and are sailing along the edge of a massive volcanic wall that looks like a fortress in the middle of the sea. It is the outer wall of Deception Island. There's a large, rugged hole in the dark rock which looks as if a cannonball has been fired through it. The bitterly cold wind that greets me proves too much; it makes my eyes water to such an extent I can hardly see the storm petrels and albatrosses flying near the ship. It's like looking through a rain splattered window rather than through the lenses of my own eyes. Lovely weather for storm petrels—they seem to be in their element in icy, windy weather. Perhaps that's why they're called storm petrels. I decide it will be more comfortable on the bridge.

No, I'm not a wimp, just being sensible! I promised my sons I wouldn't do anything stupid!

Along with finding my sea legs, I've also found an appetite that I'd never have believed possible. It's hard to tear myself away from the windows of the bridge as cruising around the outer walls of a volcano is not an everyday activity. Reluctantly I make my way to the dining room and pile my plate with bacon, scrambled eggs, croissants (I won't tell you how many), muesli, fruit and yoghurt. I need to refuel for my next adventure which is to become a member of the prestigious 'polar plunge club'. Breakfast over, it's back on deck as we continue our cruise along the rocky walls of Deception Island.

Deception Island, one of the South Shetland Islands, is a ring-shaped volcanic island. It is nothing like any volcano I've seen anywhere else in the world. When I visualise a volcano, the image I see is of a snow-capped cone rising out of the ground like a giant sandcastle, maybe a plume of smoke wafting from its crater and set against an azure sky. I suppose this image stems from living in Japan for over two years, where images of Mount Fuji are ever present. The most memorable one is of Fuji-san (Japanese name) towering into blue infinity, covered in snow with cherry blossom in the foreground; the whole image being reflected in Lake Kara-guchi-Ko. No plume of smoke though, as Fuji-san is dormant.

We have been told that Deception Island is an active volcano; I assume we'll land on a beach and climb up to the crater to peer into the sulphurous red hot, bubbling lava. How wrong I am! Instead of hours of hard slog over barren rocks and scree, then having to put crampons on to climb over the snow and ice to the summit, we sail gently into the crater and float over the top. I wouldn't have thought it possible. Now I know differently. The volcano's summit in Deception Island collapsed to form a caldera with a narrow entrance which was formed when the wall was blown away in an eruption allowing the sea to rush in and fill the crater. The entrance, which is 1,800 feet across, is guarded by a sheer, protruding rock that looks like a tower that might be inhabited by a giant in a fairy story. It's home to a colony of chinstrap penguins not giants and is known as Neptune's Bellows, but it is often referred to as Hell's Gate because of its precarious entrance and the ferocious winds that frequently blow across the entrance. Once safely through Neptune's Bellows, the sheltered bay is as calm as a mill pond. The name 'Deception' originated from its 'hidden' entrance. Circumnavigating the island, it appears to be a circular land mass of solid rock. That is deceptive as this is only the view when you are at a certain angle; when you've almost gone past it that you can see the narrow entrance leading into the sea filled caldera.

"What's a caldera?" I ask. I'm told it is a crater that is larger than a mile and a half in diameter, which has formed when the middle portion subsides in one massive block, enlarging the original crater. This often happens after a particularly violent eruption following a long period of the volcano being dormant. I suppose before the eruption it was an archetypal, round volcano with a high wall and a hollow centre with hot lava bubbling up from the crater.

I watch enthralled as the ship inches her way through the narrow entrance and drops anchor in Whaler's Bay just to the right of the entrance. Its name dates back to the whaling and sealing days of the 1820s when the island was claimed by the British. We are told that the volcano last erupted in 1967, but they don't *think* it will erupt today. Some comfort knowing the unpredictability of the geology in the region. At every twist and turn some remarkable facet of nature reveals itself to us. One of the first things that strikes me is that it is completely devoid of any colour. The sun is hiding somewhere up in the grey, overcast sky casting an eerie light on the patchwork of the black and white landscape. The sea mirrors the tones of the sky and the beach is dark grey, almost black.

Antarctica slips easily between extremes: from blue skies to blizzards; from tranquil landscapes to the thunderous roar of an iceberg toppling over, or a piece of a glacier calving off; from a penguin sitting next to you in trusting companionship, to seeing it being snatched in the jaws of a hungry leopard seal; from mirror flat motionless seas to being tossed about by precipitous waves; from towering icebergs to fiery volcanoes; from lonely silence to the chatter and camaraderie of like-minded people. We never know what we will experience next.

Our trusty Zodiacs land us safely on the volcanic sandy beach. The landscape is a monochrome of dramatic beauty; the crater walls are stark, black basalt rock rising to a height of 2,000 feet and criss-crossed with brilliant white snowy stripes resembling a zebra. It's like looking at a black and white photo that has come to life, and we are all part of it. This stark landscape is home to seals, penguins and whales. In one place the rock has been blasted away in the rim of the wall by volcanic bombs when it erupted. This is the gap that looks as if a cannon ball has blasted through it. It is known as Neptune's Window. With a little imagination it resembles a window that you can climb up to and look through to its precarious, sheer drop on the other side.

We are given free rein to explore, or just sit and observe the antics of the wildlife, mainly sea birds, chinstrap penguins and fur seals. I'm standing on the beach trying to decide what I should do first. I feel a bit like a kid in a toy shop wanting to look at everything at once. After standing in the snow watching the penguins and seals for about ten minutes, I decide to climb up to Neptune's Window; not an easy feat in rubber boots that are slightly too big for me. I eventually make it to the top unscathed. Two chinstrap penguins are perching precariously on rocky ledges below. They seem perfectly content and unperturbed by the sheer drop. As they can't fly, I presume they just throw themselves into the water when they want to leave the ledge, but they must have great difficulty getting up there in the first place.

Looking back along the beach to where I'd previously been standing, the bird's-eye view puts a different perspective on the old buildings as well as on the sea-filled crater. I'm able to get a better view of the shape of the crater and volcanic walls by looking down on them. It is not symmetrical as it appeared to be at sea level cruising round it. The buildings look like old toys that have been left in the garden for several years and not been played with, except by the elements. There is a cluster of dilapidated, wooden buildings that are home to fur seals. We are told not to go in them, as they are not safe. There are huge rusting oil tanks which were used for storing whale blubber and refining it during the whaling days. There is also an old aircraft hangar. Unlike other bases in Antarctica that have been renovated or completely removed, the whaling station has been left untouched except by the elements. It is an open-air museum in the care of nature's curator, but probably also with a little help from the United Kingdom Antarctic Heritage Trust. There used to be a single engine Otter plane outside the hangar which was used for transporting goods. It had to be hurriedly rescued when news leaked out that someone was planning to remove it and sell it. It was considered a high value item due to its historic importance even though only the fuselage remained. The base was also used as a landing place for the first flights over Antarctica.

In 1929 Admiral Byrd, a US Naval Officer, polar explorer and pioneering aviator, was the first person to fly over the South Pole. Following this experience, more than anything he wanted to be alone to experience absolute peace, quiet and tranquillity. In 1934 he set out to achieve his mission. He went to Antarctica with a small group of scientists, starting off from their base called 'Little America'. They travelled inland some considerable distance from the base and erected a hut for Byrd to live in which they called 'Advance Base'. Once it was made habitable, the scientists returned to Little America, leaving Byrd alone. He spent six winter months completely alone, living in a hut with just one small stove for heating; a scant source of warmth in -70°C temperatures. He carried out weather observations and in the beginning all was well. In his book *Alone*, he describes living in such inhospitable circumstances that the cold and darkness gradually depleted his body and mind. His room was dark and non-dimensional; it was a life of physical, mental and emotional suffering, his life hanging in the balance when he nearly died of carbon monoxide poisoning from fumes coming from the stove. His loneliness was too great for him to take lightly and he often questioned why he was there and what he was doing. Thankfully he lived to tell the tale.

Deception Island has long been a sight of scientific research, beginning with the British claiming sovereignty in 1829. It was occupied by British scientists and sailors until 1908 when it was leased to the Norwegians for 21 years for commercial whaling. It was abandoned in 1967 following volcanic activities which caused high seas and considerable damage to the base. All personnel were saved, but some of the buildings and the whalers' cemetery were swept away in a flood of water, mud and ice. Two solitary crosses remain with Norwegian names engraved on them. One is so worn away by the elements that it is impossible to make out the name on the cross; the other is very clear and bears the name, 'TØ MMERM HANS A GULLIKSEN'. He was a Norwegian carpenter who died on 4 January 1928.

The isolated cemetery on Deception Island

What is their story I wonder? It's unlikely they died of starvation with such an abundance of food on their doorstep; or of old age as I doubt older men would have been sent to Antarctica for such a tough job as whaling. I don't know what sort of medical facilities they had, but I shouldn't think that major surgery would have been possible. There must have been numerous accidents in the course of their work, so maybe fatal injury was the cause. While I'm pondering their fate, fellow passenger Susan joins me and we speculate about possible causes of their deaths. We come to the conclusion that an accident or a lack of medical facilities was the most likely cause.

This leads Susan to tell me a story about her extraordinary medical dramas while working at the Amundsen-Scott base at the South Pole. She says she volunteered for the Advanced Trauma Team to work alongside a general practitioner and a 73-year-old surgeon as part of their emergency preparedness drills. They performed three successful operations at the South Pole: an appendectomy, a hernia repair and excision of an external growth. Her role was circulating surgical nurse and lab technician. She tells me about how the doctors thawed chickens from the freezer for her to practice closing wounds and different suturing techniques. I presume the chickens provided dinner that night (minus the stitches I hope). The appendectomy ended up being rather complicated surgery and part of her task was to monitor the patient round the clock for a full week while he was being weaned off painkillers and other medication. I suppose an operation like that would have been impossible for the Norwegians who lie beneath the sand and snow on Deception Island. Listening to Susan's story makes me feel very much in awe, and very much more in touch with the reality of life and death in Antarctica.

Susan tells me about the lighter side of life at the South Pole. She says that according to records kept at the Amundsen-Scott base, she was the oldest woman to overwinter at the South Pole and also the oldest person to be inducted into the '300 Club'; a rite of passage when the temperature hits -100°F. The sauna is stoked up to 200°F in order for people to soak up the warmth before streaking out to the Geographic South Pole marker and back, in temperatures of -100°F. Susan says that at the South Pole her oxygen levels hovered at around 90 per cent, but for the first three months they were closer to 85 per cent. It took a long time for her body to acclimatise, as in effect she was at an altitude of 14,000 feet with thin air. She says even climbing the stairs left her breathless. Walking around outside in temperatures of -90°F with five to ten knot winds, and wearing 25 lbs of cold weather gear added to her breathlessness. Walking slowly with frequent breaks was the only way she could breathe. I look incredulously at her, lost for words. The expression on my face leads her to say that a winter at the Pole is an amazing experience - certainly not something she'll ever forget. But it was a very long nine months living in the dark, isolated from the rest of the world along with 48 other cold souls. What a vibrant, adventurous character Susan is.

The polar plunge club

While we are enjoying exploring, Geoff and Shane get to work digging pools in the volcanic sand near the water's edge. This is to be our reward for our 'stupendous act of bravery', not only swimming in the icy waters of Antarctica, but risking life and limb sharing it with leopard seals. They've got big, menacing looking reptilian heads, and long necks unlike other seals whose more rounded heads and faces appear to grow out of their bodies. Leopard seals have a spotted coat and large pectoral flippers. They are a massive 12 feet long and weigh 1,300 lbs. The female is larger than the male. They're much bigger than the other seals that inhabit Antarctica. They eat krill, fish, penguins and crabeater seals. They are inquisitive animals, but can be dangerous. They've got teeth like crocodiles and have been known to eat humans! Actually there has only been one known death at the whim of a leopard seal. The person who was killed was not eaten. It was a young woman named Kirsty Brown, who was working at the British Antarctic Survey station of Rothera, south of the Antarctic Circle. She was drowned on 22 July 2003 while snorkelling as part of her research work into seagrass. It is thought that the leopard seal was just playing with her and pulled her down into very deep water causing her to drown.

After several hours of exploring it's time for what is the highlight of the day for most of us; to become a member of the prestigious, elite 'Polar Plunge Club'. I strip off my lovely, protective, warm clothing and don my bikini. I run straight into the cold, silver-grey sea with a mixture of great excitement mixed with trepidation. I feel an overwhelming desire to just sit on the edge for two seconds and then rush out, but ego plays a big part in it. To be able to brag "I've swum in the Antarctic Ocean", or "I've swum in the crater of an active volcano", spurs me on. I also have a very stubborn streak, once I've made up my mind to do something, I don't like to back out. I run into the sea and gasp as the water washes over my skin. I don't dare venture in too far, in case a leopard seal is looking for its breakfast, but I immerse myself briefly and splash around for a short time. I'm very aware that I might have to make a quick getaway if I need to. Nearly all the passengers take part in the plunge. It's a surreal experience swimming around in the crater of an active volcano and sharing it with the cute, local inhabitants. I have never heard of any other volcano where creatures and people swim around in its crater in air temperatures of -15°C. The locals have no manners though; they're just staring at us unashamedly in amused curiosity before getting bored and waddling off, or hauling themselves into the cold sea to show off their swimming skills. They probably think we are a species of lily-livered weaklings, so they want us to see

Immersion in the thermal pool

how much tougher they are. Show offs! Native swimmers have fur or feathers and most have a thick layer of blubber, so a prolonged swim in the cold sea for them is normal; it's a bit like wearing a wetsuit. I would stay in for much longer if I was wearing a wetsuit. It's nice for humans to know that they are the underdogs to wildlife for a change.

"Phew, it's hot!" When I packed my bikini I had no idea that Antarctica could be almost unbearably hot. Not that I'm complaining—it's sheer bliss lying in a hot pool gazing at the icy beach and mountains. Of course I was expecting the sea to be very cold, but what I'm not prepared for is how hot the water in the pool that Geoff and Shane have dug would be. It's almost harder to lie back in the hot pool than in the cold sea. I gradually acclimatise to the steaming water as it penetrates through to warm me to the bone. It's bliss! It's much better than a sauna. How relaxing it feels to lie back in the hot water, gazing at the bleak, snowy landscape all around us, while at the same time watching my fellow travellers taking the plunge, observed by the seals waddling along the edge of the sea, or poking their snouts out of the water to get a better view. I can see why Admiral Byrd said he felt as if he'd been plumped upon another planet!

While I'm lying back soaking up the hot thermal water, I'm soon joined by two young, good looking, male skinny dippers. They are fellow passengers, Thorfin and Van, they sit either side of me. My lucky day! For some the water is too hot, so Geoff has to wade into the sea and fill up big plastic bags full of cold sea water to tip into the hot pool. Unfortunately all good things must come to an end, and all too soon it's time to get dressed and let the Zodiacs zoom us back to the ship. We nose our way between Neptune's Bellows and head south into calmer waters near the mainland.

7. PURE ICE

It is our expert glaciologist, Alex, who tells us how ice can be as diverse and interesting as everything else in the universe. Alex has a zest for life and adventure which has led to him travelling and climbing all over the world. He's a true Canadian patriot, quite understandable given the beauty of nature in Canada. He tells me the Rockies and Antarctica are his favourite places on the planet. He says he fell in love with the Antarctic continent because of its history, wildlife, incredible landscape and general other-worldliness. I have fallen in love with Antarctica for the same reasons. Alex has worked in Antarctica on numerous occasions in support of science for the British Antarctic Survey (BAS) and US Antarctic programme.

I feel like a three-year-old whose most used word is "Why?" I wonder what makes a glacier move. Why doesn't it remain in the same place like the ice sheet covering the rest of Antarctica? My questions are soon to be answered. In his presentation accompanied by a film, Alex takes us deep into the heart of a glacier, right down to the bedrock where melting water has carved out gleaming white and blue caverns and luminous pools of water. All these images are accompanied by the sound of dripping water, the tone changing according to the depth of the pool, the drops echo like music around the icy walls of the cavern. They trickle down the stalagmites of ice and fall into the pools in a rhythmical plip plop, their percussive, echoing resonance is magnified as it bounces off the freezing walls of the glacier making an eerie timpani, like metallic musical instruments in an orchestra. I feel as if I'm actually there in the glacier with him, I can even feel the icy cold as my nostrils inhale the clear air.

Ice has many contradictions: it is transparent, but glows with colour. It is ephemeral and can melt away in the blink of an eye, but it can be thousands of years old. It is fragile but has the strength to grind away rock with the same power as modern machinery. It can change from pure white to deep blue in the cracks and crevasses with an almost endless variety of shades of white inbetween—forty shades you may say. It is made up of intricate, jagged hexagonal ice crystals which deflect sunlight in all directions so it looks white, but close up it looks transparent. Ice crystals absorb light at the red end of the spectrum, but when sunlight penetrates deep into the ice, only blue light is reflected back. At the heart of an ice crystal are molecules that are held together by bonds which are constantly making and breaking. When the temperature drops to zero they begin to hold, forming a pattern that holds the bonds far apart causing numerous air bubbles, which is why ice floats. Although it looks dense, the air opens it out making it lighter than water.

Alex informs us that Antarctica consists of 5.5 million square miles of frozen land that is almost entirely covered in ice. Glaciers are formed by layers of fallen snow, they become like a frozen river of ice running down the mountain valleys. They have deep crevasses reaching down to the bedrock below. Although they are solid ice, they are moved along by gravity and the sheer weight of the ice, but the movement is imperceptible to us. The only movement we can detect is when the glacier reaches the end of its journey to the sea and great chunks calve off. First you hear a rumbling sound like thunder, and then there is a creaking sound followed by a massive chunk of ice calving off. The body of ice appears to crumple from the base like knees giving way when someone faints. The ice cries out with the weight of its body with an almighty crackle like the sound of gunfire in a war zone, this is followed by a splashing groaning sound as it hits the water and rushes to get away; the energy building to tsunami-sized waves, the size being dependent on the amount of ice that has split off. The bergs are top-heavy and irregular in shape, which along with the underwater melting, causes them to lose bulk under the water making them top-heavy. This makes them topple over from time to time and rise higher in the water. They also growl ferociously when they topple over. They often form incredible blue and white ice sculptures in the sea.

"What the ice gets, the ice keeps"
(Frank Worsley, Antarctic Explorer)

Glaciers are one of the most powerful forces in nature. They can carve through rock, sink ships and engulf heavy objects the size of a double-decker bus, the ice freezes over them as if swallowing them whole, leaving no trace of their previous existence.

After World War Two a Lancaster Bomber was converted to a passenger plane and flew people across the Andes from Buenos Aires in Argentina to Santiago in Chile. In 1947 the pilot was following his usual flight path across the mountains and calculated his position as being close to landing in Santiago. Unbeknown to him, he had been blown off course and his miscalculated position caused him to crash into one of the highest mountains in the Andes range. Despite search parties scouring the mountains, the wreckage was never found. Its disappearance remained a mystery for 50 years. The crash had caused an avalanche that completely covered the plane, swallowing it deep inside a glacier. The movement of the glacier carried the plane to the end of its journey where it finally emerged after 50 years of being buried deep inside the ice. This disturbing image and Alex's words have a powerful effect on all of us, so what better way to end the experience than to go on an ice tour.

Cierva Cove

Due to the weather and sea conditions our schedule has to be flexible, we are asked to listen out for announcements. We have an early dinner at 6.30pm. and prepare to go out for a Zodiac cruise in Cierva Cove, a beautiful little sheltered bay on the western side of the mainland. To make the most of the evening light, it's all speed to put on our thermal underwear, flip our tags and board the Zodiacs. We don't need to disinfect our boots; in fact we don't need to wear boots as we won't be landing. There doesn't appear to be a landing beach in the vicinity, only the sheer cliffs of the actual mainland of the continent. There's nothing but icebergs everywhere. We set off in the last golden rays of the setting sun which are reflecting off the glistening white ice. It's one of the most breathtaking and memorable journeys I've ever made. Words fail me as I tour round this indescribable landscape of ice. Fortunately others have already described the scenery more eloquently than I can. The following is a quote in which Frank Worsley, Shackleton's captain on *The Endurance*, describes the amazing shapes and images one can see in icebergs.

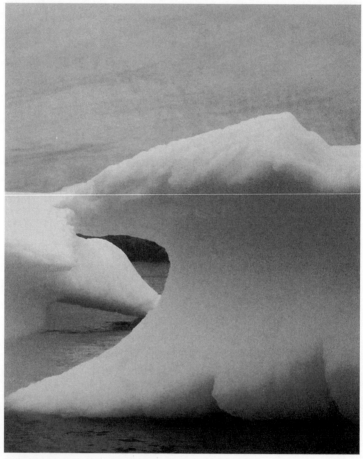

Ice sculpture, on its way to becoming a 'mushroom'

Swans of weird shape pecked at our planks, a gondola steered by a giraffe ran foul of us, which amused a duck sitting on a crocodile's head … all the strange, fantastic shapes rose and fell in stately cadence with a rustling, whispering sound and hollow echoes to the thudding seas.

The mainland is made up of typical dark volcanic rock pushing through the thick ice sheet that covers it. We cruise around some of the most pristine and fantastically shaped icebergs imaginable. They surround us wherever the Zodiacs take us. It's like a beautiful garden of ice sculptures that has been carefully set out by nature's hand. We cruise past bluish-white ice mountains with cavernous entrances that appear to be lit by fluorescent light; a kaleidoscope of ever changing colours ranging from transparent to crimson. As the evening light starts to fade, the cave entrances become dark and mysterious. There are tall towers with blue stripes round them, making them look twisted and contorted. Some are massive walls of ice with weirdly shaped sculptures on the top. Others are like icy, jagged mountain peaks with wide, glowing, cobalt blue stripes running downwards from on the top, they look like luminous veins of blue blood trickling down shiny white skin. The blue stripes are similar to the blue crevasses in a glacier, but very smooth instead of the jagged deep furrows in a real glacier; these icebergs were part of a glacier once of course. One very memorable one looks like a camel lying down—the top of its head and ears clearly defined above its long face; a slightly disjointed jaw makes it look as if it's chewing something. It has one big hump between the base of its neck and rear end. It couldn't have looked more realistic if a top sculptor had been commissioned to sculpt it. There are sea fields of large, icy white 'mushrooms' dotted around, they look almost edible.

The sky is a pearly blue, streaked with pink and liquid gold light. It reminds me of a description in a book on Zen art that I once read. A Japanese artist was trying to paint a sky in his picture. No matter how hard he tried, it didn't come out the way he wanted it to. In exasperation, he picked up a cup of sake (Japanese rice wine) and took a mouthful, but he didn't swallow it; instead he spat the sake over his paper, like a venomous viper.

Then in anger he flicked his paint laden brush at the paper. To his amazement, there before him was the perfect sky. I don't know if he finished the flask of sake to celebrate, or gained momentous incentive to continue painting. This story perhaps explains how the sky at Cierva Cove came to look so beautiful.

I was very interested in the technique that the Japanese artist had used and tried it out myself. While I was living in Japan I collected and pressed lots of different flower petals, leaves and the wings of a few dead butterflies I'd found lying in the streets of Tokyo of all places. When I returned to England I decided to make them into a picture. I took a mouthful of water and spat it out over my paper; then I loaded my brush with blue paint and flicked it over the paper. Disaster! After several attempts I decided the water was to blame. I opened a small bottle of sake I'd brought back from Japan with me. It worked! I flicked blue and white paint on it and got a beautiful sky of different shades of blue with white streaks and puffs of cloud. I had no idea nature and sake could be such good art teachers. However, it doesn't always work—if you try too hard, it lets you down; it has to be spontaneous, just like nature.

A newborn weddell seal

We see a newborn baby weddell seal lying on a bergy bit and mum is keeping a watchful eye while lying on another bergy bit nearby. A bergy bit is the small remains of melted sea or glacier ice which had once been a large iceberg. Both seals look at us with huge dark sad eyes. I wonder how anyone could look into those eyes and club them to death to use their fur for coats and accessories, purely for financial profit. Killing for survival is a different matter when you are hungry, but then any predator whether human living in the wild, or animal will only take what is needed. Seals were hunted to near extinction in the past. When will we humans learn that everything on the planet does not belong to man?

Dusk is falling, but the sky still retains its luminous pearly light, but the blue streaks have turned green, and the pink have become purple. Highlights of gold still shine through. It's a bit early in the season to see the *aurora australis*, but this is still an incredible sky of dancing light. We stay out till nearly 10:00 p.m. even though darkness is closing in. A rather scary, eerie shadow flits under the Zodiac making us stare nervously into the water. To our amazement we are about to be given the opportunity of watching a water gymnastic display performed by a leopard seal. It repeatedly emerges alongside the Zodiacs, sticking its long, reptilian head as high above the water as possible, then disappearing under the Zodiac, sometimes emerging on the same side, and sometimes on the opposite side. It keeps looking at us as if to make sure we are still watching. I think its game of hide and seek has been deliberately planned to keep up our interest and attention. It's as if it's saying "You've done enough ooohing and aaahing over icebergs, now look at me." The more I watch these marine animal and penguin antics, the more I become convinced that they are sensitive to human appreciation just as we are.

We reluctantly make our way back to the ship still followed by the leopard seal frolicking in the wake. Leopard seals are supposedly solitary creatures, but this one seems to be enjoying a bit of human company. I find it hard to believe that they might kill people as I watch this friendly, harmless looking seal; it seems to want to be our friend and play with us not harm us. We return to the

A friendly leopard seal plays in Cierva Cove

ship as dusk is wrapping its crepuscular dim light across the sky. The ship's lights are blinking eerily between the ice sculptures and the darkening sky.

As we cruise gently past these impressive icebergs and gaze at the jagged mountains covered in snow, interspersed periodically with glaciers that are rutted with deep, blue crevasses, it seems inconceivable that this land was once covered with trees, plants and animals. Fossils have been found dating back 250 million years. Some of Scott's 1910–12 Polar party discovered fossilized ferns in Antarctica which are only found in the other southern continents of the world. They also found the fossil imprint of a tree.

8. THE BIRTH OF ANTARCTICA

I try to visualise this icy landmass stripped bare of its frozen white cloak and covered instead with exotic plants and trees. It is impossible to see such a picture in my mind: it would not be Antarctica anymore, it would lose its uniqueness making it just like any other continent. So how was Antarctica born?

Birth is often referred to as the everyday miracle. The birth of Antarctica, in fact the whole universe, is as much a miracle as the birth of every living creature on Earth. The stories surrounding the birth of the universe are as diverse and varied as any science-fiction tale; whether myth, religion or science. There are so many differing opinions as to how the planet came into existence, but the Old Testament, and subsequently also the Christian creation theory, is the one most of us know best. In this creation theory, God created the heavens and the world in six days from nothing. As the Old Testament has it he also made the stars, the heavens, the seas, and the land that became the Earth and all living creatures.

I'm not a scientist, in fact I've never studied a science subject other than human biology; I'm only going by what this Antarctic journey has inspired me to dig deeper into. What I understand of the Big Bang theory is that the universe came into existence a little over 13.5 billion years ago, by a massive explosion from a single point of infinite density at an incredibly high temperature. Subsequently this cooled and expanded into the universe we know now. This, for understandable reasons, has been difficult to prove and the search has been on for evidence to prove, the 'Big Bang theory' with attention focused on a particle known as the Higgs Boson that should exist according to the theory first postulated in the 1960s by Peter Higgs, a physicist at the University of Edinburgh. But it had never been found. It is also known as the 'God Particle'—to the irritation of many scientists—because if real, it seems to support the idea of one original event—creation if you like—at the beginning of everything.

There has recently been a breakthrough in scientific discovery; it is believed the existence of the Higgs Boson particle has finally been confirmed following experiments conducted using a massive machine called the Large Hadron Collider in Switzerland.

In some respects this version of the Big Bang theory seems to be very similar to the biblical creation theory in that it describes a single explosive event that gave birth to all of creation. Our planet and everything in the universe including the Earth, hence began as formless, primordial matter without order or arrangement before it gradually took shape or was shaped. Later liquid, molten rock from 4.5 billion-year-old asteroids collided and the molten rock hardened to form a solid mass. Asteroids are boulders composed of rock and some metallic elements floating around in space; they are known as meteorites if bits break off and fall to earth. Such a rock or meteorite that contained ice which melted and became water, may some scientists think have provided the building blocks for life on earth.

Some creationists believe Big Bang science is proof of a God that is the origin of all things, whereas others (young earth creationists) treat the Bible as literal truth, evolution as false and both life and the earth as coming into being only between 5,700 and 10,000 years ago. In this respect the idea of 'building blocks' of life from an explosion billions of years ago and later via meteorites is rubbish. Either way science and religion do perhaps agree that life is miraculous and extraordinary.

Whether either form of creation theory or Big Bang theory is one you believe to be correct, it still poses the question – who made God? And was there really such an abrupt transformation from 'nothing' to everything? There are so many things we cannot know for sure and questions we cannot answer.

But what about the birth of Antarctica? That is still to come. Mythology has also played a big part in explaining how the earth came into existence. I'd like to tell you a lovely little mythological story about the birth of the islands of Japan, a story I was told when I spent a week in Hokkaido and visited an Ainu village.

In the past the aboriginal people of Japan, the Ainu, who live on the northern island of Hokkaido, believed in animism, the bear being the symbol of the cult. Until quite recently they were hunters and fishermen but their race is more or less extinct now. The name 'Mount Fuji' is from the Ainu language and it is probable that Ainu superstitions were the foundation of the Shinto religion in Japan. The present day race came from the Asian mainland and regarded themselves as descendents of superhuman beings called Kami. In the eight century AD two chronicles – the *Kojiki* and *Nihon Shoki* recorded the mythology of the origin of the Japanese race. At the beginning of time there were several deities, the most important being Izagani and Izanami who gave birth to the islands of Japan. Izanagi gave birth to the sun goddess, Amaterasu, and the storm god, Susanowono-Mikoto. The sun goddess was the ruler of the Plain of Heaven, and the storm god was ruler of the Sea Plain. He had a violent nature and lost his temper which frightened his sister who shut herself in a cave, plunging the world into darkness. All the other deities tried to entice her out of the cave by putting a mirror outside the entrance. They then started dancing and laughing loudly; the sun goddess's curiosity got the better of her and she peeped out from the cave. The first thing she saw was her own reflection in the mirror; this enticed her out of her hiding place. The world was returned to light and warmth again. The storm god was expelled from heaven, so the world could never return to darkness again.

The Japanese myth is no longer considered to be literal truth, but up until the end of World War Two, the Japanese royal family were considered to be descendents of the sun goddess.

We have the birth of the idea of Antarctica from the Greek philosopher Aristotle (384–322 BC); it is based on the idea of a harmonious world of balance. He suggested that there was a large unknown land mass in the south to counter the land mass in the north. Long before the days of exploration this idea was very much part of the architecture of his thought rather than a proven scientific fact. As it so happens of course, his idea proved to be far from mythological, but it took many centuries to pass before this land was actually seen by explorers.

Aristotle thought that everything in the universe was in balance and maintained an essential symmetry. In astronomy *Ursa Minor* (Little Bear) is the most northerly constellation which also includes Polaris, the one fixed point in the northern sky above the North Pole. This constellation is above the Arctic landmass of Siberia, Alaska, Canada, Greenland and Scandinavia. Aristotle thought there must be a land in the Southern Hemisphere, *terra Australis incognita*, (the unknown land) to balance the known Arctic lands in the Northern Hemispheres.

True to Classical Greek symmetry, in the second century AD, Ptolemy the Egyptian astronomer, geographer and mathematician, also thought that the North Pole landmass must be balanced by a South Pole landmass, so the idea of a continent at the southern end of the world was consolidated. In the Greek language *Anti* means opposite and *Arktos* means bear. The unknown continent immediately opposite the North Pole constellation of Ursa Minor, which means Little Bear in Latin, became known as Anti-Arktos. Most people know it as Antarctica. Despite never having been seen by either philosopher or scientist it was not a mythical land. It was therefore in a curious way the beginning of the age of rationalism rather than otherworldly mythology that provided the first explanation for Antarctica's existence. The North Pole constellation isn't a myth either, but there is a lovely mythical story about how it came into being.

There are several legends surrounding Ursa Minor, the most popular interpretation is the Roman myth that Ursa Minor was Arcas, the son of the very beautiful Callisto. She was turned into the great bear Ursa Major by the goddess Juno, who was very jealous of her beauty. Callisto wandered around in the woods for many years, and then one day she saw Arcas in the woods. Overjoyed she ran to greet her son who was out hunting. He recoiled in horror and was about to kill his mother with his bow and arrow, but Jupiter intervened. They were both removed from the earth and sent to the sky as celestial bears and became known by their Latin names, *Ursa Minor* and *Ursa Major*. This has many similarities to the myth regarding the islands of Japan.

Knowledge is a wonderful thing, but does it have the side effect of inhibiting creative thinking and a sense of wonder about our existence?

The geophysical birth of Antarctica

"Nothing exists but atoms and the void; it is not emptiness,
but the uncreated that precedes all creation, the beginning
of the potential of all things."
(Democritus)

The Earth is about four and a half billion years old. Three hundred
million years ago the land was joined together in one superconti-
nent known as Pangaea. This period commenced in the Palaeozoic
era when there was a proliferation of plant life. Tectonic plates
in the outer portion of the earth's crust, the lithosphere, are still
continually moving causing earthquakes, volcanic action and
mountain ranges to form. This movement of the plates causes continents to collide; Pangaea was formed in this way, but they also
cause continents to drift apart. Two hundred million years ago in
the Triassic period, when dinosaurs first appeared, Pangaea split
into two continents; the northern hemisphere landmass became
known as Laurasia and consisted of North America, Europe and
Asia. The southern hemisphere landmass was known as Gondwanaland and included Australasia (Oceana), Africa, India and
South America. Eventually these two landmasses started breaking up about two hundred million years ago resulting in six of
the continents we know today. It was a very gradual process as
tectonic plates move only two centimetres a year, twenty metres
in 4,000 years. There are seven continents not six; so where was
Antarctica? At that point it didn't exist. The main body of what
we now know as Antarctica was joined to Australia, and the tip
of the Antarctic Peninsula was joined to the tip of South America. It finally broke away from Australia towards the end of the
Cretaceous period about fifty-five million years ago, but retained
its link with South America; a grip which was as tenuous as the
fingers of two friends clinging tenaciously to each other, reluctant
to let go. Approximately twenty-two million years later the fingers
slipped from each other's grip and Antarctica drifted south.

Following the scientific work carried out by Captain Scott's
men in 1910–13, the theory of continental drift of the two
super-continents of Laurasia and Gondwanaland was supported

91

when Edward Wilson discovered a fossilised plant specimen in Antarctica called Glossopteris. This discovery supported the link between Antarctica and the other southern continents. Glossopteris is an extinct seed bearing tree that existed during the Permian Period and flourished on Gondwanaland. It became extinct in the Triassic period. It is one of the species of the genus *Glossopteridales* which has been found in South America, Africa, India, Australia and Antarctica and was confined to the southern hemisphere. From studies carried out on its leaves and from the deposits in which it was found, it is thought to be a deciduous plant. The leaves are up to a metre long and tongue shaped, hence its name which means tongue. Three other geologists on Scott's

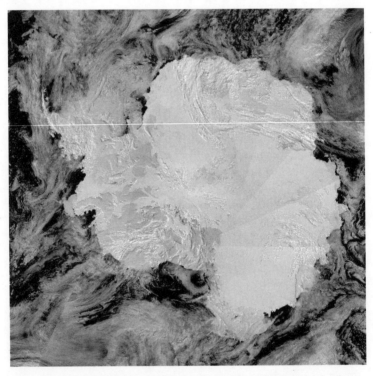

Antarctica as captured via NASA's Aqua satellite on 27 January 2009. Under the ice and weather patterns not many features of the landscape are visible.

expedition, Frank Debenham, Raymond Priestley and Thomas Griffith Taylor, studied the geology of different areas to discover more about the composition, geological evolution and the age of the continent. They collected thousands of specimens, including fossilised ferns, trees and other plants establishing further links to Gondwanaland.

It's hard to think that great continents can drift around in the ocean. Perhaps the word 'drift' is not a suitable word to use; it conjures up an image of something floating on the surface of the water and moving slowly on the ocean currents. In reality the continents did not float, but were forced to break up and move away through tectonic plates colliding or separating. The continents are of course, firmly fixed to the sea bed unlike the ice sheet that breaks up and floats on the ocean currents.

Geologically Antarctica is divided into sections, its average elevation is 8,000 feet with mountain peaks pushing their way up through the ice sheet—they are known as nunataks. Greater Antarctica is the eastern section, making up the largest and highest portion of the continent, it is almost entirely above sea level; it consists of rocks that are more than 570 million years old. It would be even higher if it wasn't for the weight of the ice pushing it down. Lesser Antarctica is the western side of the continent and has a different terrain from the eastern side. It has a coastline in some places, many islands in the channels, and mountainous terrain which includes the Antarctic Peninsula. The Peninsula is an S–shaped strip of land that is a continuation of the Andes, the mountain chain that stretches for about 4,500 miles down the spine of South America. The distance between Cape Horn and the tip of the Antarctic Peninsula is approximately 690 miles. The Andes mountain range developed as part of the Ring of Fire a chain of volcanoes encircling the Pacific Ocean. The chain has the highest mountain outside the Himalayas, Mt Aconcagua in Argentina at 23,034 feet. Mt Erebus is Antarctica's most active volcano. Greater and Lesser Antarctica is separated by the Trans-Antarctic Mountains which are one of the longest mountain ranges in the world at 2,000 miles long.

The Central Region is the Polar Plateau, a vast plateau rising to 9,900 feet above sea level. The highest mountain is Mt Vinson at

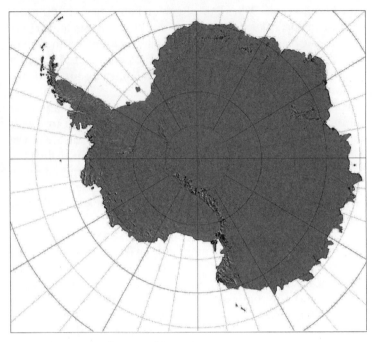

Composite mosaic satellite map of Antarctica

16,863 feet and situated at 80°S. The geographical South Pole is located in this central region. The ice sheet is so thick it fills the valleys between the mountains which would normally be below sea level without the ice. The ice sheet began forming between twenty to twenty-five million years ago, reaching its greatest extent about five million years ago.

At this point in my voyage of discovery I am totally unprepared for the astonishing richness of Antarctica, from its wildlife, geology and history, to the more recent scientific work carried out leading to a greater knowledge of the planet. Before my Antarctic journey I had never even heard of Pangaea or Gondwanaland. I used to feel ashamed if I didn't know about things that some of my friends seemed to be very knowledgeable about. This journey is changing that. I'm no longer ashamed, it's so interesting that

I want to know about it for the sake of my own soul, not to be clever and show off my knowledge. All these discoveries are very enriching and some are also entertaining. Whale watching comes into the entertainment category.

9. A WHALE OF A TIME

The same as every morning, Geoff's calm, reassuring voice wakes us up. We are having a lie-in this morning; it's 8.00am. After breakfast most of us go on deck or to the Bridge. Spouts of water like fountains are spurting up in every direction, a sign that the whales swimming alongside us are about to breach, which is when they leap out of the water and then dive back in. Once again my camera is working overtime. I suddenly see what looks like a fountain coming up from below the sea. I hold my camera at the ready but it's very difficult to track where the whale is going to emerge, then have time to aim, focus and shoot. Just as I click the button I feel sure the whale has disappeared below the water. I think I've got a lot of pictures of the sea and nothing else. An animal in constant motion that keeps disappearing into the foaming depths is not the easiest subject to capture on film even with the best camera in the world, and endless patience is needed of course.

We gaze hypnotised by a massive humpback whale that breaches the water over ten times as it swims alongside the ship. It's really showing off its acrobatic skills to the enthralled audience. I wonder if whales are conscious of the effect they have on us, and if they have an ego too. It seems as if this wonderful performance is being executed with the intention of giving a show stopping performance. We all like praise and to be appreciated, maybe animals do too. From the moment I see the head rise up out of the water, my eyes are glued to the sea waiting for a repeat performance. I am finally learning the skill of being able to track approximately where a whale is going to breach by the tell-tale fountain, which is rapidly followed by a gigantic knobbly head rearing up from the depths. It almost looks as if it is smiling at us as it propels its massive body skyward before arching and diving back into the foaming sea leaving behind the iconic image of its great fluke (tail), which seems to hang suspended, pointing upwards for ages. Sometimes they thrash the water with their flukes before submerging and disappearing into the depths of the ocean. They look almost the same size as our ship, but although humpback whales look massive, they are actually the fifth largest of the whales. Blue whales followed by fin whales are bigger. humpback whales weigh up to 45 tonnes. Males are shorter than females, about forty to fifty feet long compared to females which are two to three feet longer. They have a dorsal hump, black knobbly head and long flippers up to sixteen feet long. Their name comes from their habit of humping their backs when they dive. They have a unique pattern on their fluke, (the word for the tail of a whale) which is unique to each individual whale, a bit like finger prints for humans.

I definitely feel as if I've been driopped on another planet as I watch these amazing mammals showing off their skills. It isn't just the visual display that grasps my attention; it's also the knowledge I am gaining from our leaders about this wild land and its inhabitants. I'm not only seeing something new for the first time; it's a true revelation of 'seeing'. Understanding more about the nature around me is a valuable part of my personal journey. It has opened up a whole new world of which I previously knew very little despite travelling extensively. A whale has ceased being simply a whale as I learn that flukes are tails with no skeletal structure; humpbacks blow five to ten times and then submerge for up to twenty minutes; they can swim at nine to ten knots and hunt in pods of four to six whales. Their acrobatic skills are thrilling, particularly when you take their great size into consideration. They can jump right out of the water, and then lob tail, which is when they beat the water with their tail and flippers.

Humpbacks are not just exciting acrobatic performers; they are also the opera singers of the whale world. They sing to one another, making the longest and most complex sounds of any animal. If you listen carefully, you might hear the music of the sea – the songs of the humpback whales, sopranos, baritones and tenors – discordant sounds to equal the musical innovations of Stravinsky.

A Whale of a Time

Diving: an acrobatic humpback whale

Geoff has travelled to Antarctica over eighty times; I ask him if he still feels excited when he sees the wildlife. He assures me he does, each time is as exciting as the first, but he also enjoys seeing the pleasure and excitement that we all feel.

Not to be outdone, gentoo penguins are also playing a game of 'now you see me, now you don't'. They almost fly out of the sea; skim the surface about a foot above the water before diving under again. It's a well choreographed and well rehearsed performance, all executed amongst a backdrop of icebergs, glaciers, blue sea and marine wildlife. We are also entertained by an albatross, its great wings arcing gracefully as it flies along with us for a while. There are a number of black-bellied storm petrels that accompany us as well. The sun eventually decides to grace us with its company creeping tentatively across the grey sky as if it's not sure whether it should venture out or not. As whales are such a focus at the moment, we avidly look forward to the talk our Marine Biologist, Ingrid, is about to give.

Beached

Ingrid's love affair with the sea began early – her family sailed around the world on a 57 foot yacht, leaving when she was just sixteen years old; they lived on the boat for four years, covering 52,000 nautical miles.

Arriving back in New Zealand, Ingrid completed three university degrees: a BSc in Zoology, an MSc in Marine Biology and then spent eight years on research for her PhD, studying orca, (aka killer whales) in New Zealand waters.

She is totally obsessed with orca, and has worked with New Zealand orca for over fifteen years. The Orca Research Trust was founded by Ingrid in 1998. It is the first research project dedicated to orca in the South Pacific. It is now working in association with other research groups and has expanded into other areas such as Antarctica, Papua New Guinea and Argentina. Adopt an Orca was founded in 1998 by Ingrid and it was the first whale or dolphin adoption programme in Australia. It was set up to facilitate educating the public about these amazing animals and to help raise funds to promote orca research. Ingrid is also a surf lifesaver, a diving instructor and has her captain's ticket for working on ships. She has worked in both the Arctic and Antarctic on numerous occasions. She also writes books for children.

As a marine biologist and whale researcher, Ingrid's passion for the work she does is obvious. She tells us how there are various theories as to why whale stranding happens. For example, it could be because the whales are fleeing from a predator, they lose their sense of direction, they are about to give birth, they are sick, or they are committing suicide. Ingrid's talk focuses on mass beaching in particular, rather than a lone whale being beached. One theory is the possibility that they are like lemmings: if one does it, they all do it. Apparently lemmings don't do that in real life—allegedly they got the reputation for this behaviour when they were forced to jump over a cliff during the making of a film. I don't need reminding not to watch it.

Ingrid shows us a documentary film about orca in New Zealand. Orca are members of the dolphin family, but they are much longer at twenty-six to thirty feet compared to a dolphin at about seven feet. They usually inhabit coastal waters and feed in groups—they even kill and eat sharks and other whales. Females give birth every three to ten years and suckle their young for about a year. Ingrid's work has focused mainly on getting beached whales back into the sea. In mass beaching there is a key whale, and if that whale gets beached, the others in the pod follow. They form a sort of daisy pattern around the key whale, like a centre surrounded by petals with the key whale in the centre. The rescuers pour water over them to keep them cool, and dig holes around their flippers to make them more comfortable. Their flippers normally face slightly forwards, but when they get beached, they often face backwards. This is very uncomfortable for the whales and by digging holes it releases the flippers so they can return to their natural position. Whales know when a person is trying to help them and will roll onto their sides to make it easier for their helper. They also raise their tails to help with the lifting process which is carried out by placing mats under the whale as supports to lift it. They are given fresh water to drink so they don't have to use up vital metabolic energy converting their normal sea water into fresh water. Once the rescuers have got the key whale back in the sea, they rock and roll it to stop it swimming in circles, then they turn it to face the other whales who will follow it back out to sea. From this it appears that the mass suicide theory is erroneous, but I don't think marine biologists are any nearer to finding out for certain why beaching happens.

Ingrid's presentations are so memorable and easy to follow; as with the other expedition leaders, I can't believe how lucky I am to have the benefit of travelling with such kind and interesting people.

At the beginning of our journey, just before our first landing in the South Shetland Islands, one of the most important rules we were told was not to let any plastic bags blow away that we are using to protect our camera equipment. Apart from it looking awful, we are made very aware that a floating or beached plastic bag could be very dangerous to wildlife, with these often being swallowed whole by marine mammals mistaking them for a jelly fish. This is brought home to me very vividly when Ingrid tells us about a very sick whale she and her team rescued. It was not in a pod but had beached alone, at first the team could find no reason for its acute bad health. After a long process of examination they discovered a small piece of plastic poking out of its anus. The poor creature had swallowed a plastic bag and was unable to pass it out, so it was blocking its gut. When the rescuers managed to remove it, it passed out a pile of rotting squid and other fish. Fortunately it fully recovered a few days later, but if it hadn't been rescued, it would certainly have died. Unlike humans, whales give birth feet first. If they give birth head first it is called a reverse breach birth, often leading to the death of both mother and baby. The gestation period of a whale pregnancy is between ten and sixteen months depending on the species. A whale foetus of one month's gestation looks more completely formed than a human one at the same stage. I remember when my daughter-in-law, Justine, had her first scan at three months pregnant. Sophia, my granddaughter looked like an oil slick on a moonlit sea—at least that's what the image looked like to me. She was hardly recognizable as a human at three month's gestation. However that image was probably more to do with the fact that it had been downloaded onto her computer, then copied and pasted and sent to me by email when I was living in Chile. I'm sure the picture on the screen in the hospital would have shown a fully-formed human foetus because nobody seemed concerned.

I wonder why a human foetus develops so much more slowly than a whale, especially as human gestation is only nine months, while a whale takes one to seven months longer. Maybe it's because a whale has to survive and swim amongst predators from the moment it's born. Even though it stays close to its mother all the time, it's still very vulnerable. A human is protected and nurtured in a 'safe' environment for several years before becoming semi-independent. Once again I am left pondering things that I've never thought about before.

10. A PHENOMENOLOGICAL JOURNEY

"In the obscurity of the midday twilight we carried Lieutenant Danco's body to a hole which had been cut in the ice, and committed him to the deep. A bitter wind was blowing as, with bared heads, each of us silent, we left him there ... And the floe drifted on."

Henryk Arctowski, a Polish geologist.
Belgian expedition 1897–9

At 6.15am the intercom system crackles into life and Geoff's voice says "Good morning everyone, it's a beautiful day in Antarctica. We will be landing on Danco Island in thirty minutes." After a quick cup of coffee and a croissant, we set off on our first early morning landing of the day. Danco Island is a small island one mile long, lying just off the Antarctic mainland in the narrow Errera Channel at 64°'S. It is named after a Belgian geophysicist, Emile Danco, who was a member of the expedition team on board the ship *Belgica*. The *Belgica* set out from Antwerp in 1897, under the command of Adrienne de Gerlache, to carry out scientific surveys in Antarctica. Roald Amundsen was one of the team. Danco died of heart failure while on board the *Belgica* in Antarctic waters and was buried at sea.

Dawn is breaking, holding the promise of a clear sunny day ahead as the Zodiac glides across the water. It is pure magic watching the first light of day creeping across the sky. Light and dark playing a game with each other as if trying not to wake anyone up; subtle hues constantly changing to embrace the new day. The remaining mist still clinging to the surrounding landscape, is beginning to creep away to be eaten up by the ice and snow. The sun is rising over Mount Français, a 9,055 foot mountain peak of almost vertical rock on the mainland; it seems as if the sun is trying to reassure us that it hasn't disappeared for the imminent winter months that lie ahead. It glistens on the peaks of Anvers Island to the west, crowning them with a liquid gold halo of incandescent light, wisps of cloud drift across blue sky. It is other-worldly in its magical beauty.

Danco Island was occupied by the British from February 1957 to 1959 and known as Base O. The British hut was removed in 2004 after the Environmental Protection clause was added to the Antarctic Treaty in 1998; it stipulated that all buildings had to be either maintained or demolished. In the case of Danco Island absolutely everything was to be removed, leaving no trace of human habitation or activity. I certainly can't see any sign that anyone has even landed here before us, let alone lived here. There aren't even any footprints in the snow other than those belonging to the penguins. Apart from the whaling station on Deception Island, there's no evidence that anybody has been to Antarctica before us.

No man or woman has been here before me, I am the first. This is a phenomenological journey where reality is a truth in the mind of the individual rather than an external, general truth. Of course people have been here before—the stories of Scott and Shackleton and Amundsen are etched on most people's minds, but it's the first time for me. David Livingstone is credited with discovering the Victoria Falls which he named after Queen Victoria. The fact that the native dwellers of the land called it Mosi oa Tunya (The Smoke that Thunders) and had known it for thousands of years was apparently of no consequence to Livingstone and Europe. And so likewise I have discovered Antarctica!

As we land we are greeted by our 'hosts', a group of Gentoo penguins and a few fur seals. Most of us climb up a steep bluff which is 590 feet high. It is covered with icy snow making it very slippery to climb. The views from the top are worth the effort. The landscape is out of this world: mountains covered with snow and tinged with early morning light; an almost translucent blue sky and sea in the Errera Channel, the latter dotted with glistening white and blue icebergs and bergy bits that look like silent ghosts or spirits from the past.

I feel an overwhelming sense of belonging in Antarctica; this is my heritage. It is as if I've always been here, it has become part of me, a timeless experience without language or reason. I simply 'am', just like my surroundings. There's no need to question or analyse the world. Being here is enough. I'm experiencing the 'now'. There's no past, no future; it needs no explanation or projected meaning or understanding. I sit with penguins in the snow in companionable silence; they are just as much part of this incredible panorama which is spread out before me, enveloping me in this awe-inspiring nature. I have a strange feeling of nothingness, like a statue—not moving—here forever, no notion of time. How long have I been here? I don't know. It doesn't matter. All I know is that I am far more alive and eternal than in the kind of somnambulist state I tend to experience when trudging through daily life, where routine obliterates the senses, blindfolding me to things around me, my actions becoming so automatic they are performed without conscious awareness, and are definitely seldom memorable. This experience of Danco Island is like being part of an atmospheric painting that expresses so much it is alive, yet nothing moves, time stands still. There are no words that adequately describe it. The commonplace objects of ordinary life have been transplanted by a new existence. I'm as insubstantial as ether, but never more alive.

What a change from the stark, black and white landscape we saw at Deception Island which has an entirely different kind of beauty; perhaps more dramatic in its stark monochrome scenery compared to Danco Island's serene, aesthetic beauty. The visual stimulus is not the only sense to be aroused; I now know the sound of silence. It's all around, like a stereo system blaring out not sound but a silence in which you can hear a pin drop. It's not a lonely silence, it's a peaceful silence, there are people and penguins all around, but nobody speaks. What use are words in such a landscape? Even if there weren't any other people, it wouldn't feel lonely I'm sure. How can I feel lonely when I'm at one with nature; an integral part of it. I feel I belong to it as much as the snow, the mountains, icebergs and wildlife. I'm free of all earthly, social constraints.

These views and feelings are images I often now visualise when I'm stuck in a traffic jam or feeling low. They lift my spir-

Danco Island

its instantly. The extremes of Antarctica are then to me at their most powerful, from flourescent blue sea to liquid gold light; from the reality of a known continent with scientific bases to the unreality of simply being there; from living for that moment as in childhood, to now being a grandmother transported. Nothing has changed in the decades that have passed between my childhood self and my grandmother self. It makes me realise that I am the same person I always was as far back as I can remember. I'm ageless, 'child' and 'grandmother' are just words with an external meaning, they have no definition in the reality of simply being.

I have just joined a select few of mortals, not because I feel superior or better than others, but because I have experienced the life force within myself, of being an eternal part of where I am, a reality of the moment. Far from feeling proudly aloof, as joining a higher cult of mortals might suggest, I feel humbled and in absolute awe of my surroundings and nature. Antarctica is a word to be whispered again and again, like the sound of the wind in the trees, or the name of a lover you long to be with. It holds magic that can take you out of yourself and into other ways of being.

Oneness

Exploring new lands and carrying out mapping and scientific work was not the only exploration in the quest to slake the thirst of the enquiring mind. For hundreds of years philosophers have been seeking for the meaning of life and many different theories have been postulated, but the rationalist philosopher, Rene Descartes (1596–1650), was one of the most influential and regarded as the inaugurator of modern philosophy. His main idea was that consciousness cannot just exist by itself as an objectless state of mind. His thinking was somewhat mechanical, as if the mind and reality were like a machine that can be controlled, totally rational and devoid of feeling. Science, as we know it today, didn't exist in the seventeenth century, so Descartes thought that there was no indubitable way of acquiring knowledge. He became fascinated by the question of whether there was anything we could know for certain, not something that was just a state of mind. He tried to find propositions which could not be doubted. The only thing he knew for certain was that thinking definitely existed, hence his famous saying 'I think therefore I am.' Then along came the German philosopher Edmund Husserl (1859–1938). He came up with a completely new theory of reality, which is that we are not just subjects knowing external objects, but our feelings and experiences are also important. This new theory is known as phenomenology, which comes from the Greek word, *phainomenon*, to show or that which appears. It is the science of phenomena, but it isn't a science in the usual understanding of the word where a theory is tested and repeated again and again to verify the same results each time. It is a philosophical enquiry into intellectual processes which are characterised by the exclusion of any preconceived ideas and causes, unlike scientific analysis which revolves around observable, external reality. Phenomenology is purely concerned with whatever it is that's experienced and real to the individual independent of any outside reality. It became the fore-runner of existential thinking.

My journey is the pure description of my individual experience and my own reality, which may be completely different from other people's reality of Antarctica. It sets aside any preconceptions regarding existence I may previously have had. It is not important whether it is objectively as I experience it; it is purely personal to me. Husserl said 'We are beings in and amongst and inseparable from a world of being.' My experience in Antarctica has made me think and feel more deeply about this idea than I have ever thought before, and has shaped my need to write about my experience to share with others.

I found a kindred spirit in Admiral Richard E. Byrd. He wrote about his personal, phenomenological experience of living alone in Antarctica, in which he refers to his dawning of awareness and understanding of philosophy. He wrote:

> I was learning what the philosophers had been harping on about – that man can live profoundly without masses of things. For all my realism and scepticism there came over me,

Oneness

too powerfully to be denied, that exalted sense of identifica-
tion-of-oneness-with the outer world which is partly mystical
but also certainty … There were moments I felt more alive than
at any other time of my life. (*Alone*)

My journey in Antarctica isn't proving to be a sudden dawning of awareness; it's a gradual unfolding of awareness of the
planet and my place in it. Each day of my journey reveals some
incredible facet of nature and history. My experience of being in
Antarctica is another kind of revelation about myself as much as
the world I live in. Whilst the television programmes on Antarctica are incredible, particularly the amazing photography, and
they are also interesting and informative, the one thing they can
never capture is the feeling of levitation you get when you're actually there. It transcends all the other senses and anything I've ever
experienced before. Walking on air isn't a myth; I'm not gravita-
tional, but levitational. That's how I feel in Antarctica—that same
incandescent glow, as real as the rising sun, at peace, an eternal
enduring life force that has made me part of it all.

As Jean-Jacques Rousseau said, 'Man is born free but is everywhere in chains.' Here on Danco Island I've broken those chains,
perhaps only for that moment, perhaps forever.

The return

Reluctantly we have to turn our backs on this remarkable experience and head down to the waiting Zodiacs. Most of us slide down
on our bottoms, which break the magic spell, but it's a good fun
way of getting back to a different reality. It takes me back to my
childhood camaraderie with my friends, when we all shared in
the excitement of playing in the snow and sliding on icy puddles.
I feel the freedom of that moment slipping away as I hurtle down
my slippery descent. Several years later, while putting it all down
on paper, I try to think of other times when I've been lost in time
with no external reality. I can only compare this experience of
oneness to love making; when you are no longer aware of the self,
but totally one with your partner with whom you are entwined.
No restraints, a free body and soul lost in another world, another

time, a primordial act of nature. In a strange way childbirth is similar—I was completely lost in the experience of bringing my two sons into this world in just the same way, nothing else existed but us and that moment.

My exalted sense of identification-of-oneness with the outer world is only a transient moment outside time. Back on board it's back to mechanical time, breakfast is served at 8.30am and while we are eating, the *Shokalskiy* repositions in the Errera Channel and fortunately we have plenty of time to eat before we enter Neko Harbour.

11. THE ANTARCTIC MAINLAND

"Glittering white, shining blue, raven black, in the light of the sun the land looks like a fairy-tale. Pinnacle after pinnacle, peak after peak, crevassed, wild as any land on our globe, it lies, unseen and untrodden."
(Roald Amundsen, South Pole expedition 1911)

Our ship glides into the harbour across an infinite, placid surface studded with glistening ice, the sunlight scattering it into thousands of sparkling fragments. The furrow left behind by the ship's passage soon healing over and returning to its previous equilibrium, leaving no scar. We make our first landing on the mainland of the Antarctic continent. Previously we've only landed on islands. The views across the harbour stop me dead in my tracks; it is unlike any harbour I've ever seen before. When I started writing about Neko Harbour I decided to ask a few people how they would define the word harbour. The following are some of the words people said "Safe haven, busy, bustling, quayside, gangplank, fishing boats, pleasure boats, crowds of people, and fog horns". Ours is the only boat we've see on the entire trip.

On one side of Neko Harbour dark brooding perpendicular cliffs rise up out of the mirror calm sea, dusted with fragments of ice glittering in the sun on the surface of the intense blueness. The highest peak is 9,200 feet. Sometimes light cloud drifts across the mountains leaving only the jagged peaks appearing to grow out of the cloud creating a mysterious feeling of being in a heavenly universe. On the other side of the harbour huge glaciers slowly make their way down to the sea, streaked with shiny, blue and white ribbons of ice decorating the snow capped mountains. The only sound is the sound of silence. None of the defined words for harbour are true about Neko, not even the expression 'safe haven'.

Majestic Neko Harbour

If a large piece of ice breaks off one of the glaciers, it will generate huge waves that will swamp the beach like a tsunami, sweeping any living creature out into the harbour. I suppose it could be described as busy and bustling as once again there are numerous penguins waddling around, rushing in and out of the sea and jumping onto rocks. Few stand still for long. I don't know what their mission could be, but whatever it is, it must be very important for them as they seem very determined and focused on what they're doing. Some of them come up to inspect us like customs officers at a border crossing. I suppose that's only to be expected when you enter a new continent!

I sit on a rock on the beach for a while, mesmerised by the view. I'm soon joined by a gentoo penguin that jumps up onto the rock and stands next to me. Not to be left out, another comes up and stands in front of me, looking at me as if she wants to make conversation. I speak to both of them—they appear to be very interested in what I'm saying as they gaze at me intently with their heads on one side. It seems as if they're thinking about what I've just said and are considering their own opinion. But I don't think they speak English. For some reason my teaching skills have deserted me. A bit further away another penguin is sunbathing on a lump of ice. To me it's a strange thing to sunbathe on, but penguins are so well insulated that they can overheat quite quickly and need to cool down, so what better sunbed than a block of ice. Perhaps I'll try it one day! The sand and pebble beach is strewn with boulders of various shapes and sizes. The sea is crystal clear, allowing ripples of sunlight to play with the strands of seaweed on the bottom. Then suddenly a dark, streamlined image appears under the water, moving so quickly like a mini torpedo or a shadow flitting across the sun. A moment later the shadow takes form as it pops up out of the water and waddles in an ungainly fashion onto the beach.

Nearly everyone climbs to the top of a very high glacier that consists of thick, tightly packed snow, so compressed it has turned to ice. The view looking down from the top is awe-inspiring. A small group of people are standing a few metres away. The sun is glinting between two mountain peaks, the beams splitting into sharp arrows of gold light—when it touches the ground it is like a spotlight on a stage; the people are no longer people but tiny silhouettes standing out starkly against the glittering white. They are dwarfed by the surrounding scenery. I turn and gaze across the contrasting azure sea to where the *Shokalskiy* has dropped anchor.

The *Shokalskiy* looks like a child's toy that has been accidently dropped overboard from a cruise liner in some exotic far away sea and has then followed its own adventure, tossed around on all the seas of the world until it finds Antarctica. Miniscule against the towering cliffs and mountains it looks so alone, adrift and lost in an icy wilderness.

In Antarctica views are constantly changing, nothing is the same for very long, which seems strange in a land of nothing but snow, mountains, glaciers and icebergs. Once again I am lost in the oneness and timelessness of it all. However, time hasn't ceased to exist in the minds of the 'grown-ups'; we have a schedule to keep so have to make our way back down the glacier to the waiting Zodiacs. I cheat a bit and borrow a fellow passenger's ski-poles. I must say they make the descent far less scary. It means I can't slide down on my bottom though as it would be too dangerous waving ski poles in the air as I hurtle down. I have to make do with watching the others zooming down instead. My fear of sliding down steep icy slopes stems from when I climbed Volcan Villarrica in Chile at 2,847 metres. Climbing up felt safe but the descent was a different matter. We had to take our crampons off and slide down using our ice picks to slow us down. I didn't have the strength in my arms to dig the pick into the snow, so I used my heels to slow me down. Suddenly my right knee went one way and my foot the other. I was in agony and my knee was very swollen. I don't want a repeat performance of that, although the Chilean volcano was much higher than this glacier.

On the way back to the ship we're taken for a cruise around the harbour and we see two crabeater seals basking on an ice-floe. Crabeater seals are the world's most abundant seal with a population of more than thirty million. They are about eight feet long and weigh around 500 lbs. They are quite beautiful with their turned-up snouts and gentle eyes. Their colour varies from blackish to silvery grey. Contrary to their name, they don't eat crabs,

Penguins by the beach

Return to the ship passing by a crabeater seal

but feed mainly on krill. Their teeth are like a sieve that can filter the krill from the water they swallow. They inhabit the edge of the pack ice and are often scarred from attacks by leopard seals. Their main predator however are orca, which sometimes rock the ice floe backwards and forwards until the seal falls off. This is a well thought out strategy like a battle plan carried out by about six whales working together, so the poor seal never stands a chance of getting away.

I'm glad we don't witness this happening as I'd find it very distressing. I know I'm probably projecting my own feelings onto the seal as to how it must feel, but having witnessed the antics of so many marine animals in Antarctica, I'm sure they're capable of many of the emotions we feel. However, it would also have been an incredible sight which must seldom be seen by passing passengers. There's a cruel beauty in nature and the fight for survival.

We stop close to an iceberg and break bits off to eat. It's amazing to think that the ice I'm putting in my mouth is about 10,000 years old. Maybe older! We also take some chunks of ice back to the ship to have in our drinks. I wonder if the same legend applies to Antarctic ice that applies to the calafate fruit in Tierra del Fuego and Patagonia. Does it mean that by eating it I will come back to Antarctica? I hope so!

Lunch is served at 12.30am and feeling replete I go to two of my favourite haunts, the bridge and on deck. We spend the next two and a half hours or so cruising down the beautiful Lemaire Channel towards our next destination, Port Lockroy. It's a narrow channel flanked by ice cliffs made from annual snowfall and compressed ice and dusted with recent snowfall etched along the sides. These ice cliffs are interspersed with high, brooding peaks whose stark, towering beauty is in complete contrast to the lower white of the icy cliffs.

We see a tabular iceberg to starboard; it is not a towering giant like the ones we saw in Iceberg Alley, but much smaller, although it has retained its table-top shape. It must be very old as melting would happen gradually. It is in a part of the channel that opens into a wider area so Captain Kisselev very kindly takes a detour to circumnavigate it. At one end there's a tunnel of ice where the ocean currents must have worn right through, it appears to be illu-

Brooding peaks seen cruising down Lemaire Channel

minated by clear, electric blue light. It has a kind of magnetic pull as if enticing onlookers to go through the tunnel into the heart of the ice. Although miniscule by most tourist ship standards, the *Shokalskiy* is still far too big to attempt entry. It's probably one of the most photographed icebergs on the trip. It could have been a fairy-tale castle from the ballet *The Nutcracker*, when the Prince takes Clara to the land of the snowflake fairies.

The weather is still perfect without a cloud in the sky. Scanning the surrounding panorama, all I can see is glistening blue and white, a view which is not unlike our 'journey' into the deep crevasse in the glacier that Alex took us on, but this is much more spacious. What will we experience next?

12. HUMAN ENDURANCE

The morning welcomes us with a somewhat unfriendly greeting. How fickle Antarctic nature can be. Its moods are extreme; they swing from disorientating blizzards that hold no differentiation between the land the sea and the sky, to absolute clarity, well defined terrain and beautiful ice sculptures; a kind of seductive apology for its earlier unruly behaviour. It's never to be trusted—just when it's lulled you into a false sense of security, it flares up again in unabated anger. Unaware of these sudden mood swings I go out on deck to look for whales, but am greeted by the unexpected lashing from an invisible perpetrator. Frozen stiff by the cold wind I make my way to the sauna to try and warm up in time

Ice sculptures before the onset of Antarctic blizzards

119

for Alex's showing of *Behind the Scenes of the Making of the IMAX Shackleton Movie,* a reconstruction of the *Endurance* saga. Glaciology isn't Alex's only field of work in Antarctica: he provides safety and technical support for films and TV, most notably the 2001 IMAX feature film that we are about to see.

The build up to this heroic, epic adventure began in 1901 when Sir Clements Markham, the president of the Royal Geographical Society in London, asked Captain Robert Falcon Scott to lead an expedition to the South Pole, sailing on the *Discovery.* Scott chose the men he wanted to accompany him and Ernest Shackleton was one of them. On arrival in Antarctica they set about building a base at McMurdo Sound on Ross Island. After lengthy planning, three men set off to walk to the South Pole under Scott's leadership: they were Scott, Edward Wilson and Shackleton. They made it to 82°'S, but frostbite and malnutrition forced them to abandon their mission.

Several years later Scott was at sea with the Atlantic Fleet, fulfilling his Royal Naval duties. He was undeterred by previous failure and was formulating a plan to return to the South Pole. Meanwhile, Shackleton was also determined to reach the South Pole and set about raising funds to finance his expedition. In 1907 Shackleton and his men sailed on the *Nimrod* to the Great Ice Barrier in the Ross Sea, where they were hoping to land at Barrier Inlet. On arrival they found that the ice had broken away leaving a large bay which he called the Bay of Whales. Shackleton was forced to return to McMurdo Sound where Scott had made his base in 1901. He and his men built a hut at Cape Royds. In 1908 four men set off to reach the Geographical South Pole, Ernest Shackleton, Frank Wild, Eric Marshall and Jameson Adams; they travelled for 128 days without crampons, first across the Ross Ice-Shelf, which is the size of France, then over the Transantarctic Mountains, which are the same height as the European Alps and one of the longest mountain ranges in the world. They reached 88°'S, just 97 miles from the South Pole where they planted the Union flag. It was further than anybody had been before, but exhaustion, frostbite, snow blindness and lack of food forced them to return to the hut. Shackleton wrote, 'I cannot think of failure, yet I must look at the matter sensibly and consider the lives of those who are with me … man can only do his best.' He wrote a letter to his wife Emily saying, 'I thought you'd prefer a live ass to a dead lion'.

The South Pole was still up for grabs, so in 1910, Scott and his men went into action again, setting off on the *Terra Nova*, determined to reach the South Pole this time. Scott planned to take the same route that Shackleton had taken in 1907 as it was known territory, and Shackleton had got nearer the Pole than any other explorer. On 4 February 1911 six of Scott's men known as the 'Eastern Party', set off to explore King Edward VII Land and carry out scientific research. The *Terra Nova* sailed along the icy coast heading for the Bay of Whales. As they searched for a safe place to drop the six men off, they noticed a ship anchored against the ice in the Bay of Whales. It was the Norwegian ship *Fram*. One of Scott's men boarded the *Fram* and spoke to the Commander, who informed him that the Norwegian explorer Roald Amundsen had made base camp on the ice and was preparing to reach the South Pole. The Eastern Party decided to abandon their exploration of King Edward VII Land, partly because landing was difficult due to pack ice, but because they also felt that they should get back and inform Scott of Amundsen's presence and his intention to reach the South Pole. It became a race for the Pole, not between fellow countrymen, but between two different nations. Scott wrote in his diary:

> I don't know what to think of Amundsen's chances. If he gets to the Pole, it must be before we do, as he is bound to travel fast with dogs, and pretty certain to start early. On this account I decided at a very early date to act exactly as I should have done had he not existed. Any attempt to race must have wrecked my plan, besides which it doesn't appear the sort of thing one is out for.

Moods of Nature

On 8 September 1911, Amundsen and seven of his men made an abortive attempt to reach the Pole. This rather humiliating failure caused a minor mutiny when they returned to their Bay of Whales camp. They finally set off again on 19 October with dogs

pulling the sledges across the Great Ice Barrier. Their next challenge was the ascent of the Axel Heiberg Glacier, a route that was
120 miles shorter than Scott's.

On 1st November 1911, Scott and his chosen Polar party set
off on a hazardous journey that was the equivalent of going from
Scotland to the north of Spain, but in the most treacherous and
inhospitable climate in the world. The chosen men to go on to
the Pole were Edgar Evans, Lawrence (Titus) Oates, Edward Wilson and Scott himself of course. They were accompanied part of
the way by some of the other men from the *Terra Nova* whose
job it was to lay depots along the way leaving food and fuel, a
kind of larder where they left provisions for the Polar Party on
their return from the South Pole. One of the depots was named
'One Ton Depot' which they intended to lay at 80°'S, not too far
from the Pole, but the weak state of the ponies used to haul the
sledges, along with bad weather made progress slow so they laid
it 30 miles north at latitude 79°'S. That doesn't seem like much
of a difference, but as we will see, in Antarctica distance cannot
be measured in the same way that we think of distance on the
other continents. When the depot laying team were ready to head
back to Cape Evans, Scott suddenly decided to take a fifth man to
the Pole with him. He chose Lieutenant Henry (Birdie) Bowers.
His nickname Birdie came from his rather large beak-like nose.
They were making good progress but it was a land of nothing but
whiteness with no perspective and no contrasts ... until Scott
noticed a small black dot in the distance; could Amundsen have
reached the Pole before them? Scott immediately dismissed this
notion. Hope springs eternal—a necessity in times of extreme
stress and anxiety. As they trudged on, the black dot got bigger,
finally revealing itself as a flag. It had been planted by Amundsen
as a marker to show the way back on their return from the South
Pole. Scott plucked the flag from the snow and carried it with him
on a sledge.

They eventually reached the Pole on 18 January 1912, only to
find the Norwegian flag fluttering there. Scott raised the Union
Jack Flag to mark their own achievement. Roald Amundsen had
beaten them to it by just a few weeks! Not only had he left his
base to set off for the Pole several weeks before Scott, he had been

better equipped than Scott's party. Scott wrote in his diary 'Great God! This is an awful place and terrible enough to have laboured to it without the reward of priority.'

Very despondently they started to make the 300-mile journey back to the treacherous Beardmore Glacier and from there an arduous trek of 800 miles to their base camp. Unfortunately, nature's moods soon showed their vindictive side. Atrocious weather held them up and prevented them from continuing so they were marooned in their tent for days. To venture far outside would have been too dangerous. They encountered unexpected blizzards which were very unusual for that time of year. Their entire return journey was disastrous due to the unusually bad weather. It could have happened to Amundsen, but luck was on his side. They were all suffering from frostbite and what was thought to be scurvy due to not having any vitamin C in their diet. The men were getting very weak: it took them one and a half hours to put their socks and boots on in temperatures of -70°F. Sadly they all perished.

First Edgar Evans fell at the foot of the glacier; he was suffering from hunger and extreme frostbite and had lost some of his toes and his nose was rotten. How must he have felt trudging through the snow pulling a heavy sledge and negotiating crossing deep crevasses, some so deep they went down to the bedrock. He didn't regain consciousness and died on 17 February 1912. Hopefully he was unaware of what was happening. How did the others feel, I wonder, having to press on, leaving his body where it lay, and knowing they could do nothing to save him. It doesn't bear thinking about! Initially it must have been a very hard decision to make after everything they'd endured together, but a necessary one. There was nothing else they could have done other than to have given up their own chance of survival by sitting down next to him to wait for death to claim them too. They had to continue on and try and reach 'One Ton Depot' to save themselves.

The four remaining men trudged on and made camp. Oates had been shot in the leg while fighting in the Boer War in 1901, a severe injury that resulted in one leg being shorter than the other which must have hampered his ability to walk in such icy mountainous terrain. In his regiment, the 6th Inniskilling Dragoons, he had been known as 'No Surrender Oates', but sadly this horrific journey robbed him of his nickname. His intense suffering, due to the injury he'd sustained, opened up in the extreme conditions and didn't heal. He knew he'd never make it back to the depot and didn't want to hold the others up. On the 16 March, as the men were packing up the tent to move on, he asked Scott to leave him behind in his sleeping bag. Scott could not oblige. How could he have made such a decision when there's always hope? By then they knew they weren't far away from One Ton Depot and food and fuel. It had been different leaving Evans, there was nothing any of them could have done, so they had no choice. The following night they made camp, Oates hoped to die in his sleep, but this wish was not granted; he woke up the next morning. There was a raging blizzard which meant once again they were marooned in the tent till it abated. Oates pulled himself out of his sleeping bag and said to the others 'I'm just going outside and may be some time'. It was 17 March, St Patrick's Day and his 32nd birthday. Scott wrote in his diary: 'We knew poor Oates was walking to his death, but though we tried to dissuade him, we knew it was the act of a brave man and an English gentleman.' He didn't come back. His body was never recovered.

They had all suffered so much together, how must the other men have felt as they watched their friend leave, knowing he'd never come back? The three remaining men had just two days food supply left and very little fuel, but they were prevented from pressing on as the blizzard showed no signs of abating. Edward Wilson was the next to take his last breath. Even though he was near death, in his final letter to his wife Oriana, he wrote 'All is well.' He was not just putting a brave face on the situation so as not to distress his loved ones too much; he was a deeply religious Christian and knew that 'all was well' as he would soon be in the care of God and Jesus.

Bowers was next to go. Now all Scott's companions' souls had departed, leaving just their lifeless bodies. Scott knew he would soon be joining them. To hasten his end he opened the flaps of the tent to let the cold in. He opened up his sleeping bag and coat and lay with one arm across the body of Wilson while he waited for death to claim him too. The last entry in Scott's diary was on

29 March 1912. They had walked 1,800 miles and were just 11 miles away from One Ton Depot and the chance of a continued life. I suppose the only comfort the men's loved ones could take was in their heroic status and immortalised place in history. Cold comfort!

Eventually, after a period of about nine months, a search party discovered the bodies of the three men and collapsed the tent over them. A cairn was built over the tent surmounted by a cross; Scott's skis were placed at the side. They are still there today, but nobody knows of the whereabouts of Oates and Evans. I suppose their bodies will never be found unless Antarctica ever becomes free of snow. I hope that never happens. May they rest in peace forever.

Although it would have been a great achievement for the British Empire if Scott had been the first to make it to the South Pole; his real legacy is far more enduring and important. The scientific work carried out by him and his team has furthered our knowledge of the planet and pushed technology to new limits. Scott and his team carried out important scientific work such as geology, zoology, seawater analysis, glaciers and ice, meteorology, magnetic observations and mapping new terrain. His legacy has made a great contribution to science and our understanding of the planet and pushed technology to a new dimension including photography. We have Herbert Ponting to thank for that—his use of photography as a visual record of Antarctica proved to be the trailblazer for the modern wildlife photography that we see today.

Both Poles had been discovered. What next? This is where Shackleton re-enters the scene, leading to Alex's role in the making of the IMAX documentary *Shackleton's Antarctic Adventure*. Alex also appeared in the film as an extra. Not quite a famous film star—if you blinked, you'd have missed him. However, his most important role in the making of the film was not that of an actor, but of providing important safety and technical support.

Now that Amundsen and Scott had already reached the Geographical South Pole, Shackleton, aged 40, set himself a different goal. He wanted to be the first man to cross the Antarctic continent on foot, a journey that had never been attempted before. In 1898 the German explorer, Wilhelm Filchner, had set out to walk across the Antarctic and on arrival he discovered a large ice shelf in the Weddell Sea which was attached to the mainland. This was to be his starting point but he encountered serious problems. The ship, *Belgica* that they were travelling on became trapped in ice and during the long, dark winter months some of the men went insane and fights broke out. The expedition had to be aborted. The ice shelf was named the Filchner Ice Shelf after him. Shackleton decided to take the same route that Filchner had planned on doing, which was to start walking from the Filchner Ice Shelf in the Weddle Sea, a trek of 1,800 miles across Antarctica via the South Pole, and finally reach the Ross Sea. The first hurdle to overcome was to raise enough money for the expedition. The Royal Geographical Society nor the Admiralty were willing to sponsor the expedition, so Shackleton had to find private sponsors.

MEN WANTED FOR HAZARDOUS JOURNEY. SMALL WAGES, BITTER COLD, LONG MONTHS OF COMPLETE DARKNESS, CONSTANT DANGER, SAFE RETURN DOUBTFUL. HONOUR AND RECOGNITION IN CASE OF SUCCESS.

ERNEST SHACKLETON

The above advertisement was placed by Shackleton to recruit men for his expedition across the Antarctic continent sailing on the *Endurance*. Five thousand men applied.

Six weeks after their arrival in the Weddell Sea in late December 1914 the *Endurance*, under the command of the Captain, Frank Worsley, soon became trapped in pack ice and drifted north, threatening to crush the ship with its unrelenting grip. Despite numerous attempts at trying to free the ship, including the men sawing through the ice by hand with long saws to try and cut a passage through the ice, their attempts proved futile. Nobody wanted to spend the winter trapped in ice, but there was nothing they could do except drift where the currents took them with no

The *Endurance*, trapped in ice

chance of escape. Shackleton, ever mindful of the problems faced by Filchner, made sure his men followed strict discipline, but also had various recreational activities such as football, gramophone concerts and drama to keep them occupied.

Towards the end of the winter it became obvious that the ship couldn't last much longer. In October 1915 the ice began to crush the wooden hull and it started leaking; then it began to break up so they had to abandon ship. They managed to rescue some equipment such as tents and food, and also the three lifeboats and the *Endurance Spar*, the yardarm from the main mast. They spent the entire winter living marooned on the ice in temperatures of -15° F. On 21 November they watched the *Endurance* sink below the ice. They were 312 miles from the nearest land so they all knew that rescue was impossible. Realising the goal of walking across the entire continent of Antarctica was gone, Shackleton turned to a new goal of getting his men back to civilisation alive. He made the decision to march the 300 miles across the ice to Snow Hill where there was shelter. They took what supplies they could to keep them going and the three lifeboats which had to be pulled across the ice, not an easy task as they encountered numerous pressure ridges (a ridge that is formed when fragments of ice pile up in a long line) sometimes rising as high as 10 feet making it difficult to get across. They made camp on the ice floe which they called Ocean Camp. They hunted seals and penguins for food and used the blubber for fuel. For five and a half months they drifted 573 miles on the pack ice listening to the killer whales blowing nearby. The ice started to break up as the summer thaw approached and they were forced to pack up camp and set off across the ice again. They established a new camp called Patience Camp and the ice continued to drift. Suddenly a large crack appeared in the ice, and one of the men fell into the sea in his sleeping bag. Shackleton managed to rescue him knowing that he would have only three minutes to live in the icy water.

Many of Shackleton's men had dysentery and their rations were just one biscuit a day. Shackleton had to take drastic action and decided to use the lifeboats to row to Elephant Island 100 miles to the north east; at least they wouldn't be rowing against the wind. However, they had to contend with strong currents as well as a gale that swamped their boats with icy water. Sleep was impossible. It took seven days of constant rowing before they made land on Elephant Island; it had been four months since they'd touched land. Some of the men knelt down and kissed the stones. They erected tents and had their first hot meal for many days.

It was not the end of their ordeal. Five days of blizzards blew the tents away and some of the provisions; they used the up-turned lifeboats for shelter. The next problem was how to get back to civilisation. Elephant Island wasn't on a shipping route, neither was it an area that a rescue party would think of looking for them; there was no chance of being rescued. What options did Shackleton have? There were really only two options. It was a case of either spending the remainder of their lives on the island and hoping for a quick death, or trying to get off and seek help. Shackleton was not a man to give up without a fight so he made his decision. Leaving the fate of 23 of the men in the hands of his loyal friend Frank Wild, he and five crew members, Frank Worsley, John Vincent, Harry McNeish, Tim McCarthy and Tom Crean, used the third lifeboat, the *James Caird*, a 21-foot open boat, to sail to South Georgia and get help; an almost impossible journey of more than 800 miles rowing across the Southern Ocean that if you remember, sent a lot of the *Shokalskiy* passengers scuttling back to their beds in fairly calm conditions. Shackleton named the lifeboat *James Caird* after James Key Caird, a jute manufacturer and philanthropist from Dundee, Scotland whose generous sponsorship helped finance the Endurance expedition. The *James Caird* and the *Endurance Spar* are the only surviving relics from the Endurance expedition. Both items were brought back to England, the *James Caird* was given to Dulwich College where Shackleton was educated; the *Endurance Spar* is in the Scott Polar Research Institute in Cambridge.

Shackleton's group was not as lucky as us. They sailed through precipitous seas and freezing spray making them soaking wet and exceedingly cold, and a hurricane added to their misery. They eventually made it to land where they found a little cove in King Haakon Bay. After endless days at sea with no food or fresh water, even to drink must have been a terrifying experience. At least water is a life saver, even if there isn't any food available. How they survived is beyond me.

As if this journey wasn't bad enough to test the stamina and endurance of a saint, there was still more to come. Eventually, after landing safely, McNeish, McCarthy and Vincent were left to look after the lifeboat as the men were in no state to go any further. Shackleton, Worsley and Crean trekked 17 miles across glaciers, mountains and icy waterfalls to reach the Norwegian whaling station on the other side of the island. At one point they climbed up a 4,000 foot mountain only to find the descent on the other side was almost impossible. There was no way they could climb down even with ropes and their only option was to coil the ropes up and sit on them like a sledge, and hurtle down at death defying speed on their bottoms. Incredibly they landed at the bottom unscathed. All this was after all the previous ordeals they'd survived and they still had no food, shelter or fresh water. They eventually made it to the whaling station where their appearance was so bizarre the Norwegians were rather scared of them. When they realised they were human and heard the men's story, they couldn't believe that any man could have achieved such a feat. The Norwegian whalers sent a whaling ship to pick up the other three men who had landed on South Georgia. Shackleton boarded another whaler to go and rescue the men left behind on Elephant Island. Pack ice blocked his passage, forcing him to find shelter on the Falkland Islands. From there he got a safe passage to Punta Arenas on the southern tip of the Chilean mainland where the government lent him a schooner, the *Yelcho*, which was equipped for sailing through ice. The entire team of men on Elephant Island were all rescued. Not a single man had died despite the amazing hardship they must have endured. They had survived on a diet of seal bones and seaweed for 105 days.

For all the men, it was a feat of extreme bravery and endurance, made all the more remarkable that not a single man was lost; it's happy ending was the stuff of fairy tales, not reality. They were all in it together, but as the leader, Shackleton must take a lot of the credit for their survival. He put the lives of his men before anything else.

After such a death-defying ordeal, one would think that the last thing any of them would want to do would be to go back on another Antarctic adventure. In fact, the *Endurance* was not Shackleton's final journey to Antarctica. Despite being very ill, a friend invited him to go back in 1921 on the *Quest*. He couldn't resist such an offer. I can understand that magnetic pull and denial of human frailty, I suppose one always thinks "nothing will happen to me". The day after arriving in South Georgia on 4 January 1922, he had a massive heart attack and died. Antarctica became his final resting place. South Georgia wasn't just another Antarctic island; it was the place that saved his life and ultimately the lives of all his men, so it's ironic that it's also the place that took his life. Shackleton's family motto is 'By endurance we conquer'. His grave faces south-looking towards Antarctica. Every other grave faces east as in all Christian burial sites (It's comforting to know that rules can sometimes be altered in specific circumstances). In this case it was to honour an extremely courageous, caring and charismatic man who put the welfare of his men before glory. It's a memorial for all human endurance. Engraved on the back of his headstone are the words by the poet Robert Browning, 'I hold that every man should strive for his life's prize.'

Shackleton's grave, Grytviken South Georgia

In the *Endurance* film the sense of cold and hardship comes across as clearly as if I'm experiencing the drama too. Maybe there's a small part of me that would like to have the experience and challenge. That's easy to feel while I'm sitting comfortably in a modern ship complete with a sauna and good food. In reality I'd have been terrified and probably died. This film makes me feel quite guilty as I sip my red wine, sitting in a heated room feeling replete following an excellent dinner. What drives a person to have such determination and tenacity? From ancient times the human race has had a thirst for exploring the world, setting off to battle against the elements and discover what lies beyond the horizons of the vast oceans. Many, unintentionally, discovered nothing but the seabed, becoming a welcome feast for marine life in the abyss. Some of course succeeded in their quests, making and changing history.

After watching this unbelievable expedition and knowing it was a true story left most if not all of us lost for words. We sit in silence as we continue down the Lemaire Channel to our next destination of Port Lockroy, a United Kingdom Antarctic Heritage Trust base of historical importance.

13. THE UNITED KINGDOM ANTARCTIC
HERITAGE TRUST

What, I wonder, can the connection be between a naughty French nightclub, a top secret World War Two mission and a British base in Antarctica? Just before setting off in the Zodiacs to our next destination, the United Kingdom Antarctic Heritage base of Port Lockroy at 64° 50'S, we have a briefing in the bar about the history and importance of the base. It was discovered by Edouard Lockroy, a French politician who contributed funds for a French expedition to Antarctica. It is interesting to learn something about the history of the base before setting foot in the building. It creates a sense of being part of it in some way, making me feel as if I've been there before.

The British laid claim to the peninsula in 1908 but Port Lockroy wasn't occupied until 1944. A wooden hut was built, named Bransfield House which was known as Base 'A'. It was named after Lt E. Bransfield RN, the first to alight, explore and chart part of the mainland in 1820. Port Lockroy and Deception Island were both of strategic importance during World War Two, when they became bases for a top secret war mission. Sir Winston Churchill's war cabinet met to discuss what measures needed to be taken to safeguard British bases in the sub-Antarctic territories and the Antarctic Peninsula. German armed raiders were operating in the area and the Argentineans were posing a threat, as they were known to be German sympathisers. The bases were established in response to the German deployment in order to report on enemy activities and ensure the Germans were not using the harbours in Antarctica as depots, or to refuel submarines

During 1944 there was a total of 215 Naval Operations; the land based secret war mission at Port Lockroy was one of two specific operations being carried out in Antarctica; the other was the sea based party at Deception Island. The secret war mission needed a name. It was generally agreed that numbers were meaningless and therefore more secure for a top secret mission, so the Royal Navy officially named the land-based party at Port Lockroy Naval Party 475, and the sea-based party on HMS *William Scoresby* at Deception Island, Naval Party 476. The Royal Navy had taken control of Norway's largest sealing vessel, the *Veslekari*, which was commandeered to ship men to landfall points where required. The *Veslekri* was undergoing maintenance work in Portsmouth at the time and was renamed HMS *Bransfield*, leading to the suggestion that the mission should be called 'Operation Bransfield'. This code name was still not acceptable to some members of the organisation as it was thought to be a bit obvious and would provide a clue to the destination of the secret mission; perhaps the Germans would have found out about it. Unfortunately HMS *Bransfield* never made it south beyond Falmouth. It was decided that the numbers remained the best option. However, two key members of the organisation, Brian Roberts and James Wordie, felt that this 'Most Secret Operation' should have a name of provenance. In November 1943 the name 'Operation Tabarin' became official.

Bal Tabarin was, or still is, the name of a French night club in Montmartre, Paris. I don't know if the mission was named after the nightclub. If it was, I wonder why it was named after a French nightclub. There are several possibilities for its name; it was Edouard Lockroy's favourite nightclub, or maybe the secret mission was planned there. It is generally accepted that this was certainly not the case. I guess Tabarin means 'it is not what you think it is'. From 1946 to 1962 Port Lockroy continued to operate after the war when it was handed over to the civilian Falkland Islands Dependencies Survey (FIDS), which is now the British Antarctic Survey (BAS).

We are finally on our way, sailing down the spectacular Neumayer Channel that is flanked by huge ice cliffs. Unfortunately the weather has decided to make a spontaneous decision to change from the clear blue skies and sunshine of the earlier part of the day, to becoming overcast and windy when we arrive. That doesn't matter too much as most of the time will be spent inside. As we

The welcoming committee, Port Lockroy

zoom across the water towards Port Lockroy, I feel colder than I've ever been before on Zodiac crossings. Despite the fresh wind, the water is still very calm, the wind not even making a ripple. Apart from the water everything is pure white; all around, just mountains of varying heights covered in snow, enclosing us in a magic, secret circle. As we near our destination, Bransfield House comes into view, a welcome sight that stands out starkly against the whiteness of the surrounding area. It's strangely attractive and inviting. Once again I'm a little child, Goldilocks lost in the wood, when suddenly a cottage appears through the trees. In this case it's through the ice, so even more inviting. The wooden walls and roof are jet black, the roof edged with bright red paint. The windows and door are also edged with red and white paint. It is built on very rocky terrain, part of it is on a flat rocky base, and part of it is on supporting columns. There's a wooden walkway up to the door, a bit like a gangplank.

As usual on landing, we are greeted by a group of gentoo and chinstrap penguins who escort us past the Union Jack flag flut-

Bransfield House

tering in the wind, and deliver us safely at the entrance to the wooden building. Following the closure of the base in 1962, Bransfield House lay abandoned and fell into disrepair. In 1996 the British Antarctic Survey undertook a massive clean-up project. With assistance from the United Kingdom Antarctic Heritage Trust (UKAHT) and Foreign and Commonwealth Office (FCO), they commissioned the conservation and restoration of Port Lockroy. After a period of over thirty years, Port Lockroy once again became an important British base as an historic heritage site. It is closed for the winter months and opens during the summer months of November to March. The proceeds from the small gift shop pay for the operation of the sight, and any surplus goes to support other historic sites in Antarctica. In 2006 the Antarctic Heritage Trust took over the operation of the base, although it still belongs to the UK Natural Environment Research Council under the guidance of the UK Foreign Office and Commonwealth Office.

There are three people manning the base: two women and a man. They greet us as we enter and are on hand to serve in the little shop and post office and answer any questions we may have. My first port of call is the gift shop which is crammed full of enticing goodies from maps and books, to soft toys. I buy a soft toy gentoo penguin for James, my grandson, and a book on birds and mammals of Antarctica. Then I can't resist a large map, a booklet about the base and some postcards. The base is also a post office, the most southerly public British post office in the world, so we are able to buy stamps and send our postcards. About 70,000 cards are posted every year to more than 100 countries. It takes two to six weeks for postcards to arrive in the UK, as the only way of getting them from the base to their destination is to wait for a ship bound for the Falkland Islands, where mail can then be sent on. We also get our passports stamped. There are relics from World War Two days in the form of pin-up posters of glamorous girls in swimsuits. Nowadays they'd probably be topless or even naked.

I've spent enough; not only is my money dwindling faster than I'd hoped, but somehow I've got to find room in my backpack for all my treasures along with my clothes, boots, shoes and sleeping bag, and I'm not even halfway through my 'Southern Circuit Odyssey'. I'm planning to trek round Patagonia at the end of my Antarctic journey and then move on to Santiago and Buenos Aires. The shopping spree over, it's time to look round the museum. It contains a number of rooms including the living quarters of the three people manning the base, which we don't actually go into as it is home to our three hardy hosts, but we can look into the room to get an idea of what living there is like. All the other rooms are part of the museum and we're free to wander around.

Walking into the museum is like coming home from a scientific field trip, it is basic but homely and somehow familiar. It is very similar to pictures I've seen of the inside of Scott's hut, a no-frills, very lived in, secure dwelling place that is home for however long. In the museum kitchen there are some long johns, jumpers and socks hanging from a rail above the stove, on which there are a couple of kettles and various pots. The stove was originally fuelled with anthracite, as this has the highest heat output for its weight. It was probably the only place on the base where the people working there could get their clothes dry. It reminds me of my grandmother's kitchen when I was a young child; she had a rack above the stove where she'd hang my grandfather's long-johns to dry. My childhood memories are so keen, I feel as if I am back in grandma and grandpa's house. On the dresser there is an enamel bowl, several large tins of peeled and dried vegetables, Tate & Lyle granulated sugar, Chivers apricot jam, bottles of Worcester sauce, HP sauce, vinegar, pickles, salad cream, tinned fruit, Quaker oats, Marmite, Bovril, tinned kippers, strawberries and asparagus. These things are for museum display only, not for consumption by the people living there for the season. It seems hard to imagine that these things are about sixty years old; they look as if someone has just unpacked their shopping after a trip to the supermarket. I feel quite nostalgic seeing things I don't see in supermarkets very often, now own brands have taken over. Despite the harsh conditions and life of austerity, it has a homely feel about it and gives us an idea of what it must have been like to live there. In the past there was no electricity with all lighting coming from hurricane lamps, and no heating apart from the small anthracite burning stove.

The musuem kitchen

In another room there's a wooden cabinet with a wind-up gramophone on the top, and a number of old 78 records on a shelf below. The rooms are adorned with pictures, one of the Queen dating back to the 1950s and another of Prince Philip. There are also posters. One in particular catches my eye, it is of the British Antarctic Survey team standing outside the building when Port Lockroy was designated a historic site and monument under the Antarctic Treaty in 1995.

The base was of scientific importance as it specialised in geophysics, measuring the ionosphere hourly to provide long-term forecasts for radio communications. It was a key monitoring site during the International Geophysical Year (IGY) in 1957–8, when it also carried out studies of electromagnetic pulses travelling along the earth's magnetic lines of force. From 1959, it took part in a series of tests that resulted in a submarine communications system that may eventually have helped bring about a stalemate in the Cold War. It was eventually abandoned in 1962, after the research work was moved to a more modern building in the Argentine Islands, and Bransfield House fell into disrepair. Later study of data from Port Lockroy and the Argentine Islands was to lead to the discovery of 'the hole' in the ozone layer.

A team of nine men were based here during the first year of Tabarin, then an average of five men each winter thereafter. I'm told that water was scarce so only the person whose turn it was to collect and melt the snow and ice, was allowed to have a bath. Sometimes an 'inmate' would have to wait up to five weeks for a bath. Other than that, it was a place where the FIDSs could listen to the gramophone, eat, have a drink and generally relax. 'FIDS's' is the nickname the members gave themselves, stemming from usage at the time, and is the acronym for Falkland Islands Dependency Survey; people coming to work in Antarctica for the first time were known as FIDlets. Despite the name change from Falkland Islands Dependency Survey to British Antarctic Survey, the name FIDSs still survives.

In the radio room there is a 1944 B-28 radio receiver which is still in full working order; you can listen to the BBC World Service. There's also a 'clandestine' 5G transmitter. I go into the ionospherics room where there's a large glass case that contains scientific equipment which looks very complicated, full of wires, plugs and machinery. It is known as 'the Beastie' because of its innovative, but highly complex mechanism and electronics. The scientists who measured the ionosphere using the Beastie became known as 'Beastie Men'. It is thought that its unofficial spoken name referred to its legitimacy: 'B-st-rd'. I have never heard of the ionosphere before and wonder what exactly it is. I'm told if I remember rightly, that it's a region of the upper atmosphere that reflects radio waves around the world. As early as the late ninet-tenthth and early twentieth century Heinrich Hertz discovered the relationship between electricity and magnetism, which causes electromagnetic waves to behave in a similar way to waves in the sea with troughs and peaks. They are invisible to the naked eye and can travel at the speed of light curving over great distances.

Standing in this historic building looking at these instruments, I find the knowledge I'm gaining about what is happening 'up there', things I'd previously had no idea about, quite disconcerting. I'm very aware of how true the contradiction, 'the more I know; the less I know', is. The scientific discoveries are incredible, but so are the true stories of the people who discovered all this, including the likes of Edward Appleton.

Into a poor, working class family in Bradford, Edward Appleton entered the world in 1892. Despite his impoverished background, he was a young genius and won a scholarship to Cambridge University where he graduated with a double first in physics. He conducted research into measuring radio signals and discovered they were fairly constant during daylight hours, but varied at night. He was very interested in the work that Hertz, and two other men, Kennelly and Heaviside, had carried out, and their theory of a conducting layer of the atmosphere between 90 and 120 kilometres high, known as the E layer which is sporadic by nature. Appleton was intrigued by how electrical energy acted like a mirror bouncing radio waves down to Earth from different layers of the atmosphere and wanted to find out how this happened. He thought that the sun must play a crucial part in creating the electronically charged layer, as radio waves varied depending on the position of the sun and sunspots. His experiments raised more questions than answers. He discovered a higher layer 250 to 1000 high, which reflected shorter wavelengths back in both day and night, but with greater strength. This is known as the F layer (sometimes called the Appleton layer). During sunlight hours when the sun divides the denser F layer, it loses some of the reflective ability, making it harder to pick up radio signals. The lower layer is then called F1 layer, and the higher, more reflective, layer is called the F2 layer. During darkness the two layers of the ionosphere F layer coalesce, making it easier to send messages in the hours of darkness. He realised that this denser night-time layer was the best for more consistent shortwave radio communication around the world. In 1947 Appleton won the Nobel Prize for his discovery.

One of the scientists, who worked on radio waves, claimed he used to communicate with his wife through telepathy. Some people may scoff at the idea of telepathy being a reality, but as radio magnetic wave lengths were only discovered a hundred years or so ago, a very short time in terms of human existence, our knowledge, or rather scientific knowledge, is still at an embryonic stage of development in the grand scale of things.

I'm finding it so interesting. Previously I had no knowledge whatsoever about radio waves and the upper atmosphere neither did I have any interest. I'm amazed by how just a few minutes spent in this incredible museum, could have given me more insight into the world of radio waves than any amount of years spent in a class room. It is a living museum. There is a Turkish proverb which goes as follows, 'The one who travels knows more than the one who reads.' Throughout my Antarctic adventure I am finding that to be so true.

The number of ships and visitors to Port Lockroy in one day is strictly regulated, and the effect they have on the penguins is carefully monitored. Approximately 18,000 people visit the base each season. Gentoo penguins have been monitored since the base re-opened in 1996. Analysis shows that compared with data gathered from a control area where humans, other than the scientists, are not permitted to visit and they can only enter this area three times each nesting season, the breeding habits are exactly the same in both areas, so the carefully controlled number of visitors is proving no threat to the penguin's natural well-being. Regional

A healthy undisturbed penguin

environmental factors are the main driving force behind population dynamics. The United Kingdom Antarctic Heritage Trust has a high profile and Her Royal Highness the Princess Royal is the patron with a keen interest in the Antarctic. She has visited the historic huts in the Ross Sea and the Antarctic Peninsula and has written an informative foreword for the United Kingdom Antarctic Heritage Trust booklet.

All too soon it's time to leave as we're going to have an early evening barbecue on the bows of the ship, served by our excellent catering team. We don't have to say goodbye to the three people working at Port Lockroy as they have been invited to join us for the barbecue.

I leave on the first Zodiac to go back to the *Shokalskiy*. However, the weather is not being kind to us; a strong wind has blown up. We are told that the ship is moving to a more sheltered position in the channel, which means we can't return to it until it has found a suitable location and dropped anchor. I'm freezing cold because I've forgotten to put my thermal underwear on, or rather I didn't put it on because I thought the Port Lockroy building would be heated and that it was just a short trip from ship to shore. Shane, our Zodiac driver, takes us for a tour round some of the islands, we see cormorants and a fantastic reconstruction of a whale's skeleton created from old bones left from when it was a whaling station. It's massive and almost covers the small island. Although it's very interesting, I'm relieved when we start heading back to the ship. By then I'm frozen stiff, hailstones and a vicious wind are stinging my face. What a change in the weather from this morning! Antarctica is a land of uncertainty. You have to grab the moment while you can; weather conditions can change very rapidly and with little warning.

Barbecue in a blizzard

Out on the bows of the ship the barbecue is well under way. The coals are glowing red hot and the meat is sizzling, filling the air with a delicious aroma. I suddenly become aware of how hungry I am. The tables are laden with rolls and different kinds of salads, but putting it on a plate is not a straightforward job. It takes our army of passengers, chefs and crew to hold down the tablecloths, paper plates, eating utensil and some of the food to stop it blowing away. I reach out to pick up a paper plate which is immediately whisked out of my hand like a frisbee. Fortunately it lands on the deck and someone manages to quickly grab hold of it before it

Caught by the blizzard

jumps overboard into the sea. Hurricane force winds and snow suddenly leap into action within minutes. The violent wind tears at the flimsy paper plates and tablecloths, scattering them over the deck. Its fury seems to be telling us that it is incensed by our audacity at even contemplating having a barbecue on deck. Welcome to 'The Mad Hatter's Tea Party'. It's as surreal as an *Alice in Wonderland* story. Welcome to Antarctica! We've missed the moment! Once again flexibility is the key. The weather eventually gets the better of the people who are valiantly struggling to make this meal a truly memorable occasion and we are forced to beat a hasty retreat inside. Everything has to be ferried to the dining rooms. When I return home, who will believe me if I say we had a barbecue on the bows of a ship in a blizzard in Antarctica?

After dinner we are able to ask our guests more questions before they're whisked back to their remote dwelling place in the middle of nowhere, which is home for about four months. It has been a memorable but busy day, so where better to relax than the bar? A glass of red wine in my hand, I join my fellow passengers for a toast to another interesting and eventful day.

14. ANTARCTIC POLITICS AND ANARCHY

"The Earth does not belong to man."
Chief Seattle

Our journey in Antarctica isn't only about gazing at the awe-inspiring scenery, enjoying the antics of the wildlife, and visiting the most remote continent on the planet. To my surprise we are going to hear about the history and politics of this unusual continent. Politics is the last thing I would have expected to hear about in Antarctica. There are no indigenous people to claim sovereignty. It is so inhospitable that it would be impossible to live there permanently and build a thriving community. So how do politics play a part in a no-man's-land?

The idea of a southern continent as expounded by Aristotle and Ptolemy became a known reality thanks to the pioneering expeditions beginning in 1772–75 when the British explorer Captain Cook was the first to cross the Southern Ocean and the Antarctic Circle. He saw nothing more than great walls of ice and thought it was not a place worth bothering with. He headed to New Zealand, crossing unknown seas and discovered an island that he named South Georgia after King George III claiming it for Britain. Following on from Cook, Captain Thaddeas von Bellingshausen commanded a Russian naval operation in 1819 and another one two years later in 1821. He used Cook's charts to guide the expedition. In 1837 Captain Jules Dumont d'Urville, a Frenchman sailed to Antarctica under orders from King Louis Philippe to collect specimens and chart the coast. In 1840 he landed on a small group of islands and saw a new species of penguin. He named the land Terra Adelie after his wife, and the new species of penguin was named Adelie penguin. In 1839 Captain James Clark Ross crossed the Antarctic Circle. The Ross Sea was named after him. In the same year, an American Lieutenant Charles Wilkes, set off with six ships, most of which were highly unsuitable for the icy conditions, and his men were very ill-equipped. However a couple of ships made it and were able to chart a good deal of the continent and also bring back a wealth of specimens which included minerals, plants, birds and animal items. These specimens and Wilkes's log were instrumental in the founding of the Smithsonian Institute in Washington DC in 1846, a research institution for knowledge and scientific work around the world.

Pioneering expeditions into the unknown such as these sparked the realisation that very little was known about the physical properties and conditions of the Earth's atmosphere, apart from observations carried out long ago on mountains by manned balloons, which revealed the general nature of temperature and height. Later the manned balloons were replaced by balloons with self-regulating instruments. This thirst for knowledge led to scientists from all over the world deciding to make a concerted effort to work together on a plan of scientific observations to study the influence of behaviour patterns of the atmosphere in the polar regions. The agreement gave rise to the first International Polar Year (IPY) in 1882–83. There was a second IPY in 1932–33. The first meeting took place at the German Naval Observatory where the circumpolar stations of Alaska, Canada, Greenland, Norway, Scandinavia and Siberia were chosen to observe the surface elements, weather, sea temperatures and the change in temperatures with height. This required synchronised, hourly observations and absolute international cooperation. A German geologist and hydrographer Georg von Neumayer thought that Antarctica should be included in the observations

The IPY scientific work and cooperation between nations was so successful and informative that it broadened in scope to include geomagnetism, seismology, meteorology and upper air physics. An international congress on geography took place which was to determine the course of events for decades to come, leading to the formation of the third IPY now called the International Geophysical Year (IGY). Until my visit to Antarctica, I knew nothing about this important piece of history, and more than one hundred years later, I find myself drawn into these events as I listen intently to Marilyn and Geoff telling us about the International Geophysical Year and the drawing up of the Antarctic Treaty.

The International Geophysical Year (1957–8) was a quest for discovery by scientists from all over the world, involving scientists from 67 countries. It was the largest programme of coordinated scientific observations, far exceeding the previous International Polar Years in scale and scope. Following Newton's laws of motion and gravity, examination of the physical forces, actions and effects on the earth have long been a focal point of scientific observation and in particular the relationship of the Sun, the parent of the solar system and its influence on the Earth's surface, which of course is a predominant feature in our daily lives. The date chosen to begin the scientific observations was near that of a sunspot maximum, a period when activity on the surface of the sun is likely to be greater. It began at midnight on 30 June 1957 and was completed on 31 December 1958. The Arctic, Equator and Antarctic were selected for special treatment. In Antarctica scientists collected data from 52 stations and observations were made several times a day–they were known as 'Regular World Days'. Intensive observations were also made at other times when the Sun's activity was unusual. A world warning agency was established in the USA so that all stations around the world could synchronise observations of solar activity in 14 different subject areas. These included: meteorology; geomagnetism; the Aurora; the Ionosphere; solar activity; cosmic rays; glaciology; seismology; gravity and nuclear radiation. So successful were the results that, before the end of the IGY, it was decided that an additional year of this work should be performed, named the International Year of Geophysical Cooperation (YGC), to run from 31December 1959 to 31 December 1960.

Initially twelve nations signed up to it, agreeing to be united in their work and to collaborate with each other. It was a truly international endeavour for the benefit of the planet; they had open access to visit each other's scientific bases to see what work they were doing and share their findings. There were to be no secrets. Despite the Cold War between the USSR and the USA, in Antarctica the IGY enabled both countries' scientists to work together peacefully.

This collective agreement led to the Antarctic Treaty being drawn up by the original twelve member states in 1959, all of whom had participated in the IGY; the Treaty was later ratified in 1961. It is an international, non-governmental organisation set up to regulate and coordinate scientific research in Antarctica, covering the area south of 60°'S latitude. The original twelve nations that signed the agreement were Britain, France, New Zealand, Argentina, Chile, Australia, the former USSR/Russia, Belgium, Japan, the USA, South Africa and Norway. The treaty stipulates that Antarctica must be used for purely peaceful purposes, freedom of scientific research, cooperation and free exchange of information between nations. There must be no military action, weapon testing, or disposal of nuclear waste. However, military personnel and equipment may be used for scientific research. There can be no exploitation of oil, gas or minerals; all living resources such as mammals, birds and flora must be conserved. A scientist cannot take even one penguin egg or a piece of lichen for study without a permit issued by their government and countersigned by another member state. Any country is free to join, but only nations conducting scientific research can vote. There are now 46 signatories, but only the twelve original signatories, plus sixteen countries that have demonstrated their interest in Antarctica by carrying out substantial scientific activity have the right to participate in decision making. The other eighteen nations are allowed to attend. The Antarctic Treaty is the political manifesto of rules governing Antarctica, but unlike an elected political leader setting out his or her manifesto for the country, this is an international agreement in which no nation has power.

Antarctica is not completely without human habitation. Many nations have scientific bases so there are enclaves of non-permanent residents who sometimes spend several years at a time marooned in this freezing, white wilderness. No member country can claim sovereignty, but it is feared this may change with the world's diminishing resources. The Treaty neither recognises nor disputes existing sovereignty claims of the islands around the Peninsula, predating the signing of the Treaty. Some of the islands lying near the Antarctic Convergence, such as the South Shetland Islands, South Georgia and the islands off the Antarctic Peninsula have been claimed by certain nations, either on the grounds of historical discovery, or geographical proximity to their adjacent countries. However, discovery and geographical proximity alone are not enough to validate a claim without settling and governing the territory, as in the case of the Falkland Islands claimed by Britain and Esperanza claimed by Argentina.

We are travelling in the fourth IPY, which this time is actually covering two years, giving scientists the opportunity to carry out vital research in both the North and South Poles in summer and winter, as this helps the public to become aware of how the Poles affect the planet. It also enables young up-and-coming scientists to have the chance to understand how much the freezing polar regions really do influence our lives. Antarctica is the only continent on the planet where this sort of 'anarchy' reigns supreme. We now know the important part that politics plays, but how can Antarctica be equated with anarchy? Surely the very word is a complete negation of my peaceful description of Antarctica. The word anarchism comes from the ancient Greek word *anarchos,* which means without rule.

Many people think of anarchy as a purely destructive force designed to overthrow order and create chaos. We often hear from the media that a state of anarchy broke out on the city streets, cars were smashed, buildings set on fire and shops ransacked. How can this behaviour happen in Antarctica? It can't! This behaviour is not anarchy. This is a temporary breakdown in law and order, often perpetrated by disaffected groups of angry people in a divisive society, some with genuine grievances, others using the situation for the sheer empowerment of vandalism. There is still a government in power with a president or prime minister who makes the rules, even if democratically elected he or she probably doesn't represent the majority. There is also a police force to keep law and order. When so-called anarchy breaks out, it is the 'machine' that drives the system that has failed.

The idea of anarchic freedom probably seems a very negative and frightening thought when almost of us have ever experienced is living in a democratic country and being governed by a political party, but actually the word anarchism is frequently misused to dramatically describe unacceptable mass behaviour by groups of people. The *Oxford English Dictionary* defines it as 'Absence of government, disorder, confusion – doctrine that all governments should be abolished.' Apart from absence of government it is describing a very different interpretation from the ancient Greek word. I asked several people in a south coast city what they thought about living in an anarchic world. Their comments were "No way! People would take the law into their own hands. There would be piles of litter dumped all over the streets, there would be riots and nobody would be safe." Fair comment, but that seems to be the way much of the world appears to be going anyway. It seems that most of the planet is very unstable at the moment, with many of us living in fear.

The *Macmillan Encyclopaedia* which I had consulted defined anarchy as, 'A political theory advocating abolition of the state and all governmental authority.' Most anarchists believe that voluntary cooperation between individuals and groups is not only a fairer and more moral way of organising society, but is also more effective and orderly. Anarchism aims at maximising personal freedom and holds that a society in which freedom is limited by coercion and authority is inherently unstable.

As the definition states, anarchy is not against law and order and does not advocate destructive behaviour; it is based on a kind of existential philosophy which concentrates on the individual's existence in the world and it is self-governing but also aware of a moral conscience. Humans are responsible for their own actions and the effect those actions have on others, we are ultimately our own judge. As Mahatma Gandhi said, 'The ideally non-violent state will be an ordered anarchy. The state is the best governed which is governed the least.' Welcome to the ordered state of anarchy in Antarctica.

The Antarctic Treaty is based on strict adherence to rules which is surely a negation of pure anarchy. These rules have been drawn up peacefully, with mutual decision making and agreement between people of many nations resulting in the freedom of the individual from immediately imposed coercive restraint. The result is a stable and safe environment of equality and cooperation, a true state of anarchy, perhaps.

Antarctic anarchy—too idealistic? Probably, but we live in a world that is incredibly politically unstable. Even democratic countries revolve around a small group of people wanting wealth and power; a political elite that usually enforces its own will and invites little or no participation from the people who voted them in. They also frequently renege on their electoral promises, rendering the majority powerless and impotent until the next election when the whole process can be repeated by a different elite group who blame the previous government for all their failures. To quote Virginia Woolf, 'Great bodies of people are never responsible for what they do.'

If we stand back and look at our world, all nations, whether governed by a democratically elected leader, or by an unelected dictator are unfair and unstable. Maybe 'the machine' has taken over our lives removing us from the reality of nature. What next? A 'powerocracy' where the richest and most aggressive corporate empire builders take control and manipulate the 'democratically elected' puppets who only lead as far as the glass ceiling allows them to. The Japanese philosopher, D.T. Suzuki, wrote:

> The person may talk about freedom, yet the machine limits him in every way, for the talk does not go any further than itself. The western man is from the beginning constrained, restrained, inhibited. His spontaneity is not all his, but that of the machine. The machine has no creativity; it operates only so far or so much as something that is put into it makes possible. It never acts as the 'person.

I believe it was Plato who said, 'Wealth and power lead to destruction if they are not tempered by virtue.' Sorry! I'll get off my soapbox now. It's just that my free spirit and passion for Antarctica makes me like a very protective mother with her child. I realise just how insignificant I am in the grand scale of things on this vast and beautiful continent; I am just one small strand. This realisation of our place on this planet was enforced in just a couple of sentences when I read the following quote by Chief Seattle:

> This we know, the earth does not belong to man, man belongs to the earth. All things are connected like blood which unites

us all. Man did not weave the web of life; he is merely a strand in it. Whatever he does to the web, he does to himself.

Chief Seattle was born around 1786. He was a leader of Native American tribes, but he was not against white settlers and actually helped them to find land, providing they didn't take land that belonged to the Native American tribes. Their way of respecting the conservation of nature and their interpretation of God, was very different from that of the new white settlers. He made a speech contrasting the difference in thinking between white men and native thinking, but the speech was never written down, so it's a bit controversial. However, his message that man is no more than a part of nature, not nature's controller was very clear.

Following Marilyn and Geoff's talk on the Antarctic Treaty, it's hard to swim out of the deep end and back to normality. As with all the presentations I was left with a wider knowledge and a need to question what I had always taken for granted as a natural universal right. Before you think that I've been indoctrinated by two powerful anarchists, at no time did Marilyn or Geoff ever use the word anarchy in their talk: they told us purely facts about the history of the Antarctic Treaty. The peaceful cooperation between nations in Antarctica has given my mind free rein to add my own interpretation of anarchy, a theory I had used in my thesis when I was at university.

To explain, I completed a degree in related arts which looked at the relationship between art, dance, music and literature. My specialist area was dance and in particular classical ballet, using the encyclopaedia interpretation quoted above I equated ballet with anarchy. Superficially ballet, with its adherence to rules, and anarchy appear to be diametrically opposed. Ballet follows strict rules involving every part of the body and mind. After years of training I have gained physical and mental strength, balance, stamina, energy and suppleness, pushing myself to my body's limits. This has given me a feeling of freedom, a metaphysical phenomenon that has grown out of its opposite of rigid rules like a sort of endurance test. It appears to be a complete contradiction to liberation but it is this opposition which creates a feeling of balance and harmony, a 'lived' experience, not a rational thought process. Pushing my body to its limits has given me confidence and enabled me to be more adventurous and push myself to travel the world alone.

After a break for sustenance and a chance to mull over and discuss our new found knowledge, Marilyn continues with a more personal presentation about her work. She became well-known in 1995 when the National Film Board of Canada made a video documentary on her work, *Who's Counting: Marilyn Waring on Sex, Lies and Global Economics*. It was based on her book, *If Women Counted: A New Feminist Economics* (1988). The major focus of her philosophy is the idea that the current market system is fatally flawed because it doesn't reflect what people really value in their lives. She has outspokenly criticized the concept of GDP, the economic measure that became a foundation of the United Nations System of National Accounts following World War Two. She ridicules a system which counts oil spills and wars as contributors to economic growth, while childrearing and housekeeping are deemed valueless. I remember when my first child was born, I held him in my arms and gazed at him, his little fingers curled round one of my fingers, his dark eyes like soft, velvet blinked back at me. I was overcome with panic at the realisation that I could make or break this little person. The person he would grow up to be and his place in society was mainly down to me. What a responsibility!

Once again I feel so lucky and privileged to be travelling in the company of such an interesting woman. Marilyn Waring is a world-renowned political economist and she became the youngest member of the House of Representatives in the New Zealand Parliament in 1975 at the age of 23. She was only the fifteenth woman to be elected as a member of parliament in New Zealand. I've never known a person who can grip the attention of everyone in the room like she does. She's very strong minded and unwavering in her desire to help economies to grow, but without having an adverse effect on our 'home', the planet. In 1984 when she was a member of parliament in the conservative government, Robert Muldoon, the Prime Minister, encouraged visits by nuclear warships. This went completely against the grain for Marilyn and she decided to leave the party and vote in favour of making New

Zealand a nuclear-free country. This forced Muldoon to ask the Governor General to dissolve parliament and call an election. The Labour leader, David Lange, was elected with a resounding victory. Marilyn was one of the 1,000 women nominated for the Nobel Peace Prize in 2005.

Since 2006 Marilyn has been working as a professor of public policy at AUT University in Auckland and an international speaker on economic systems and how they affect the environment, and human well-being. Marilyn's presentation was most interesting and thought provoking. It has been a memorable but busy day, so where better to relax than the bar. A glass of red wine in my hand, I join the others for an interesting discussion about politics. We make a toast to Marilyn and another eventful day, and are invited to ask questions. Naturally Marilyn is faced with a barrage of pertinent questions. I feel lost for words following such a powerful presentation. Eventually the questions stop and most of us drift off to our cabins as it's getting late and it has been a long day. It's hard to sleep after such a stimulating presentation. My body is able to relax, but my mind is still very active, mulling over a lot of the points she raised. Poor Marilyn must be exhausted, but I suppose she's used to it.

15. NATURE IN EASTERN AND WESTERN THOUGHT
Petermann Island

Our wake-up call this morning is at 7.00am, quite a lie in compared to our usual early morning adventures. We wake up to a misty, damp morning with what appears to be a light drizzle enveloping the entire stark vista. As precipitation is very low in Antarctica, it's probably only the effect of the early morning mist rather than the type of drizzle we get in warmer climes. Still drowsy, I get out of bed leisurely, not fully awake.

It's like a bolt out of the blue, which I suppose it is literally. I've just washed my hands ready to go to breakfast and pressed the off switch on the light above my bed. Suddenly I find myself on the other side of the cabin with a sharp pain in my arm. I have got a small electric shock from the light. I was chatting to Libby and not looking at what I was doing, I must have accidentally touched a wire. It isn't serious but I feel very shaky, but that's probably more to do with the shock of the unexpected than the small electrical charge that has gone through me. Libby is very concerned and rushes off to find Geoff. He looks at it (the switch, not my arm) and finds nothing dangerous. He advises me to look at what I'm touching whenever I switch it on and off. A common sense piece of advice that I know I should have done, but didn't think about at the time. Mundane things are not foremost in my mind in Antarctica, as I'm living for the moment like a young child.

We are sailing down the stunningly beautiful Lemaire Channel, which is flanked by walls of very high dark rock, towering into the grey, opaque sky. They seem to be reaching up to eternity, black, gleaming rock cloaked in a blanket of brilliant white snow; soft looking in contrast with the hardness of the rock. The early morning mist adds to the other-worldly eeriness and atmosphere. I'm sure there is nowhere else on earth that is so breathtaking and

155

The brooding landscape of the Lemaire Channel

unique. It's often referred to, with good reason, the most photographed channel in the world. Luckily the weather soon clears up and the sun peeps shyly out from behind the clouds; gradually gaining a bit more confidence, strength and height, and looking down on us like a watchful parent.

After breakfast we land on Petermann Island at 65° 10'S. It was discovered by a German expedition in 1873 and named after the geographer August Petermann. We are escorted to the landing beach by a leopard seal cruising along the shore. I think he's eyeing up the gentoo penguins on the beach, trying to decide which one to have for breakfast, rather than helping us to make a safe landing, but he may be thinking we might be more of a banquet. He turns away from us deciding that we aren't worth bothering with, then suddenly there's a thrashing and splashing of water and the next thing we know, he has a gentoo penguin in his teeth. The poor little thing is trying desperately to get away—my heart's in my mouth. The gallant, courageous little bird manages to extricate himself from the sharp teeth of the seal and swims to the shore. He waddles up the beach looking none the worse for his ordeal. I think he deserves a Polar Medal. There are also a number of fur seals lying on the rocks. Maybe they would make a more substantial meal than a penguin. However, they are being sensible and staying well away from the sea. A leopard seal will snatch a penguin off the rocks, but I don't think they can kill other seals unless they are swimming in the water. Peterman Island is also home to a large colony of adelie penguins.

Adelie penguins are smaller than other penguins found in Antarctica weighing 8–12 lbs. They have a white front, black back and head and a distinctive white ring around their eyes. Their bill differs from other penguins in that it has a small, erectile crest at the top which is mainly feathered. They have a more sombre appearance than other penguins and remind me of undertakers, or waiters in a top class restaurant. They spend the winter on the edge of the pack ice and nest in large colonies of up to hundreds of thousands of birds. They migrate south in October to their own particular nesting site, which is on gentle, rocky slopes that are exposed to the wind to avoid drifting snow. They often travel 50 miles to reach their nesting sites. It always amazes me that they can find their way back and remember which their individual nesting site is, having not been back for a year. Males arrive first to claim the site. When they want to locate their partner they make a cluck-cluck-cluck-cluck sound which is similar to a bar code bleeping at a supermarket register. Their eyesight isn't very good so sound is very important. When the female arrives, the male offers her a pebble. They then build a nest of pebbles together, which is quite romantic really. During courtship and incubation neither bird eats, so they sometimes lose up to 45 per cent of their body weight. Unfortunately they are into serial monogamy rather than lifelong commitment unlike most birds; an average adelie penguin relationship lasts for no more than six years.

Just to the left of where we land, there is an emergency refuge hut built by the Argentineans in 1955. There is also a solitary cross on a mound of rocks which was erected as a memorial to three young British men who worked for the British Antarctic Survey, and who died crossing the ice. The three men, twenty-two-year-old Ambrose Morgan, a radio operator, twenty-two-year-old

Kevin Ockleton, a meteorologist, and twenty-three-year-old John Coll, a mechanic, had set off for a holiday. They decided to walk across the sea ice from their base at Faraday to Petermann Island. They were going on what is known as a 'jolly', a non-working field trip similar to a holiday and the only way of getting away from the confinement of the base. They planned to stay in the hut on Petermann Island and relax for one or two weeks, the maximum amount of leave allowed by BAS. On Tuesday 13 July 1982, they set out from Faraday hauling a heavy sledge that was laden with all their gear, including tents, sleeping bags and enough food and fuel to last for two weeks. It would take several days to walk across the ice to Petermann Island, so tents were a necessity as they'd have to camp on the ice enroute.

Every day there was constant radio contact between the three men and the base at Faraday. All was well initially, but when it was time for them to return, the sea temperatures had risen, causing the sea ice to melt. They were marooned until the sea froze over again. Fortunately there was a two month supply of food and fuel at the base hut. Not only was the lack of sea ice a problem, gale force winds and snow drifts imprisoned them in the hut. The days became weeks and still there was no sign of the sea freezing over. As the weeks dragged by their radio batteries were fading, so contact had to be limited. They were running short of food and fuel and the situation was getting desperate. Eventually the batteries died completely, and despite repeated efforts to make radio contact from other bases in the area, including Faraday, there was no response from the three men.

A sledging party from Faraday was assembled to try to get to Petermann Island and rescue them, but weather conditions made it impossible and the base commander could not put further lives at risk. Other nations were willing to help. The Chileans agreed to send out a search plane from Punta Arenas. The C-130 Hercules aircraft stopped to refuel in Tierra del Fuego before flying on to Antarctica to carry out a search of the area. Landing would have been impossible, so they planned to drop food, clothing and tents when they found the trio. There was no sign of the men. It is presumed that they tried to cross the sea ice to return to Faraday, but the ice broke up ending in tragedy. Apart from the cross on

Memorial cross on Petermann Island

Petermann Island, a memorial cross was also erected at Faraday. In October a search party managed to make it to Petermann, but the hut was empty.

It must have been very difficult for their loved ones to come to terms with their deaths, but also not knowing what exactly happened, or where their bodies lie. They were on sea ice that melted at the end of the Antarctic winter, so they may have floated away on ocean currents rather than lie buried under snow and ice on land. Perhaps they too fly on the wings of the albatross along with the dead sailors.

Despite the glimmer of promise by the partially hidden rays of the sun, the light isn't as breathtaking as that on Danco Island and Neko Harbour, as the mist continues to shroud the surrounding mountains in crepuscular light. Nevertheless, it has a cold beauty and is very atmospheric, adding to the pathos of the story of the three lost men. The terrain on the island itself is undulating and strewn with rocky hills and pools, paddling pools for the young penguins. I climb a hill which isn't particularly steep, but

Penguins on Petermann Island

in many ways is more difficult than the much steeper ones of the days before because the wet slush makes it more slippery. Most of the island is closed to visitors so as not to disturb the wildlife and meagre vegetation.

The snow is covered with low growing pink and green lichen so we are told to be careful not to trample all over it. Unlike other plant life, lichen is able to adapt and survive in the harsh, freezing conditions of the polar regions. It is a symbiosis of two separate organisms – fungus and green algae. However it doesn't resemble either of the plants. It is found mainly in maritime areas, preferring a damp climate; the lichen on Petermann Island grows on slushy ice and snow from which it absorbs water. Green algae gets its energy from photosynthesis—the pink contains phytochrome which is a pigment of green plants that exists in two interchangeable forms, one absorbing red light and the other far red light. Lichen can live for up to 10,000 years. We have been told not to walk on the lichen; it's very difficult to avoid it no matter how careful we are. I'm very aware of the responsibility all visitors have when it comes to protecting wildlife, particularly as Antarctic lichen grows only about 1 millimetre a century. I can understand why we were told not to trample on it. It also has higher antioxidants than lichens in other parts of the world which protect it from harmful UVB radiation from the hole in the ozone layer. It can tell us about the health of our environment and could possibly be used as bio-indicators of climate change in Antarctica. It looks so ordinary by comparison to some plants, but it is really quite remarkable. The terrain is very uneven and finding a way back down isn't as straightforward as going up. After clambering over rocks I often find myself unable to go any further either because of pools of water, or because the descent is too slippery. Try as I might, I can't help sliding on the lichen.

The visual 'ordinariness' of lichen makes it all the more miraculous. It's not a plant that usually stops people in their tracks to admire it. Although it is abundant in a lot of places, I've never taken much notice of it before, other than to take a photo if it

Between the darker rocks, Petermann Island's slipperly lichen

made an attractive pattern on a rock. My thoughts turn to two poems, one written by the seventeenth century Japanese haiku poet, Bashō, the other by the 19th century British poet, Alfred Lord Tennyson. Both poems are written about a little flower that each poet sees and which touches their emotions. Haiku always reflects an aspect of nature and consists of just 17 syllables – three lines of 5–7–5 syllables. It differs completely in form and feeling from Western poetry.

Unlike Western poetry, there are no rhyming words or specifically poetic feelings expressed anywhere except in the last two syllables, 'ka-na'. In Japanese this would read as an exclamation which signifies a certain emotional feeling of admiration, praise, sorrow or joy.

Yoku mireba	When I look carefully
Nazuna hana saku	I see the nazuna
Kakine kana.	Blooming by the hedge

The poem by Tennyson is a complete contrast in feeling from the poem by Bashō.

Flower in a crannied wall
I pluck you out of the crannies;
Hold you here, root and all, in my hand,
Little flower – but if I could understand
What you are, root and all, and all in all,
I should know what God and man is.

Both poems are beautiful, but to Western eyes Tennyson's poem probably seems more emotive. The difference in Eastern and Western thinking is contrasted by the late D.T. Suzuki, a professor of Buddhist philosophy and Zen in Kyoto. In his book *Studies in Zen* he lays before us the profound contrasts that arise between western intellectualism and materialism as against the Eastern concept of acceptance as the basis of the 'whole man', which is reflected in the difference in feeling and thinking in each poet. Suzuki acknowledges that both poems express a feeling of admiration for the flower, but there the similarity ends. Haiku poets are nature poets who can detect something great in small things. Bashō does not touch the flower; he just looks at it and feels the mystery of his connection with it deep in his soul. Tennyson on the other hand, pulls the flower and its root from the ground and shows no concern that it will die. His curiosity takes over from all feeling in his need to analyse and understand it, he is totally unconnected to it. Westerners are more inclined to feel separate from nature rather than instinctively feel part of it, believing it to be there to be utilised for their benefit.

When I lived in Japan, I was walking through a bamboo grove with my friend, Aiko, she told me, Japanese people consider that bamboo contains all the qualities that people should aspire to. It is upright which is seen as being honourable; it bends under pressure but does not snap which indicates flexibility; it has evergreen leaves which symbolise loyalty and it has a hollow stem which means inner emptiness. Yet another expression of the kinship between humans and nature. I doubt many Westerners would ever liken their inner qualities to those of a plant.

My feelings resemble Bashō's throughout my journey in Antarctica. I am seeing things in a new way. For the first time, I see a drop of dew glowing with colour in the sun. So often I've looked out of my window and seen the dew on the grass in the early morning, then I've looked away and carried on with my daily life, always too much to do and not enough time to lose myself in the beauty of nature. I've never stopped even for a minute to look at that drop of water and wonder at its tenacity as it clings precariously to that blade of grass. Yet it's calling out to me, "Come and see the colour in me that is refracted sunlight; come and smell the freshness of the new day; come and really see me for the first time. The Sun and I work together in close harmony to be the givers of life. We are opposites; the water can put out fire; the sun can dry up water. If the Sun dies, there will be no energy or light. If the water dies, the Earth will dry up and nothing will survive. I simply wait for you to discover me."

My journey in Antarctica has made me very aware of the intimate relationship between everything that exists, which includes not just animal and plant life, but the sea and the air and its various gases. The experience of being part of it rather than learning from a book has opened my eyes to a greater understanding of the interconnectedness of all things. We certainly wouldn't be here without all the wonders of nature, from the tiniest living thing to the biggest.

Moving away from my tottering footsteps of trying to avoid treading on the lichen, we walk to another part of the island. In one place there is an inlet of sea which forms a gully. I'm standing on the side where the ground is quite gentle and not very high above the sea level. On the other side there is a high ice cliff which is marbled with pink algae forming beautiful patterns where the snow has fallen over millennia and become impacted. Dark, swirling cracks have formed where the wind has blown in a circular motion. The cliff towers above the gentle slopes on the side that I'm standing on. It looks as stable and permanent as those other dark rocky cliffs, so it's hard to imagine that if climate change continues, there will come a time when it no longer exists. There is also a colony of adelie penguins on the rocks nearby. It's a surprise to see them as they are a little late leaving. Usually the colonies are deserted by late February. When they are swimming, their black backs provide disguise from predators from above and their white bellies provide disguise from predators swimming below.

As I start to make my way back to the beach, the slushy terrain is getting the better of me as the melted water is making the going very precarious. I fall over which makes me feel a bit shaky and I get a touch of vertigo. Not a pleasant sensation! I don't think I've fully recovered from my electric shock. Fortunately some of my fellow passengers are not very far away and can see I'm having problems. They come to my rescue which makes me feel a bit better as I have visions of falling over and nobody noticing, so my body would lie in the freezing snow until someone observed that I hadn't flipped my tag to let the leaders know I'd returned to the ship. Drama queen!

Back on board ship we reposition and head south to the Ukrainian station of Vernadsky. I'm looking forward to this landing as my friend's husband went there on HMS *Endurance* with the Royal Navy in 1993 when the base was called Faraday. The original base was built on Winter Island, one of the Argentine Islands, by the Falkland Islands Dependencies Survey in 1947. It was known as Base F and called Wordie House after Sir James Wordie, a member of Shackleton's Antarctic Expedition on *Endurance* in 1914–17. He was a geologist and chairman of the Scott Polar Research Institute from 1937–55, and president of the Royal Geographical Society. He received a CBE and later a knighthood. Wordie House is now a museum. A new larger building was erected on an adjacent island, Galindez Island, in 1954 and called Coronation House. It was renamed 'Faraday' in 1977 in honour of Michael Faraday the English scientist (1791–1867). It was at Faraday that the hole in the ozone layer was discovered. This was not its only claim to fame: it is the only base we visit in Antarctica that has a bar. It is also the base that the three explorers who lost their lives at Petermann Island were trying to reach. The Union Jack Flag was lowered for the last time in February 1996 when it was handed over to the Ukrainians for the unbelievable amount of £1.00, or so I'm told, and renamed yet again, Akademik Vernadsky. If I'd known about it, I'd have paid double the price. How wonderful it must be to claim a little part of Antarctica as mine. Of course, however much I'd offered for it, I wouldn't have been eligible to claim it as I'm not a nation that wants to carry out important scientific work there. I'm just the woman next door who is lucky enough to get the chance to come to this unique continent, but I can dream.

16. QUANTUM PHYSICS AND VODKA

At 2.00pm we arrive at the Ukrainian base of Vernadsky, the furthest point south of our expedition at 65° 15'S. The first thing we see is a big oil tank decorated with a painting of a palm tree. Is it intended to make us feel we are on a tropical island in the South Pacific? If so, I can't get my imagination to stretch that far. Anyway, I've chosen to come to the coldest place on Earth so I don't want to feel that I'm relaxing on a tropical island–also a polar plunge carries more kudos than a lazy swim in a warm, turquoise sea. There is also a signpost with the names of most of the world's capital cities pointing in the direction that they are all located in, and giving the distance in kilometres. Unfortunately I haven't brought a pen with me to note down how far London is. Oh well! I'll just have to go back and find out won't I?

Once inside the building we form small groups, each with a guide to show us around. This is a fully working base carrying out year-round scientific research. The building has been enlarged and extended, and now has two floors. From what we are shown, the ground floor is for laboratories and research rooms, and most importantly, the bar and recreation area.

My guide is Igor Gvozdovskyy, a scientific researcher in optical quantum electronics. Not only is he a very clever scientist, but his English would put a lot of native speakers to shame. He has had a very varied career and is a most interesting man to talk to. Igor graduated from Chernivtsi State University where he specialised in optical devices and systems. He moved to Kiev and continued his scientific career, entering the Optical Quantum Electronics Department at the Institute of Physics of the Ukraine. His post graduate studies concerned biologically active ultraviolet (UV) radiation and participation in the development of UV dosimeters based on solutions and liquid crystals, which are sensitive to UV

167

radiation (A dosimeter is a small device based on sensitive components which measure and evaluate the dose of UV radiation that can be absorbed by the skin).

In 2003 he went to the Vernadsky Station in Antarctica for fourteen months, where he carried out measurements with an instrument called a Dobson spectrophotometer in order to analyse the thickness of the ozone layer and UV radiation based on photosensitive solutions and liquid crystal. He was using the idea that he had proposed in his thesis. We are visiting when Igor has recently returned to Vernadsky for a second stint as the scientific assistant to the base commander. This time he is staying for exactly one year. Apart from acting as a guide to the tourists (I mean intrepid explorers), a sideline from his main work of continuous scientific experiments, he also organises scientific seminars in physics, meteorology, biology and medicine.

High as a kite

Before Igor takes us to see the spectrophotometer we learn some very interesting information about the layers that make up the atmosphere. The lowest layer is the troposphere which starts at sea level and reaches an altitude of around 10–15 miles. Above that is the stratosphere which continues to an altitude of 30 miles. Beyond that is the mesosphere and thermosphere and infinity. The Earth's atmosphere spins round with the Earth on its journey round the sun. The Earth's spin controls the weather.

In the past, observations and measurements of the earth's atmosphere were carried out in a very different way from the way they are carried out now using state of the art technology. Towards the end of the nineteenth century observations of the troposphere were carried out on mountains from manned balloons which went up to a height of about seventeen miles. It is here that the Earth's weather patterns occur. Those observations showed that the troposphere contains the layer where clouds are formed and propelled by air currents; it is characterised by turbulent processes and a variation of temperature, getting colder with height.

With international cooperation, investigation became more intensive and kites and unmanned balloons were used. These could

Igor and the spectrophotometer

reach higher altitudes into the stratosphere as they carried self-registering instruments and a meteor graph contained within an open-ended metal cylinder to protect against solar radiation. Temperature, pressure, relative humidity and the speed of air currents were measured and the data was used for forecasting the weather. It was discovered that there was a variation in temperature with increased height. They found that the variations at a rate of 6°C per kilometre in the atmosphere only seemed to happen steadily in the first ten miles of the troposphere. There was little or no variation in temperature in the stratosphere. The area between the troposphere and stratosphere where the variation ends quite abruptly is known as the tropopause. It acts like a barrier preventing the warm air rising into the stratosphere. As the warm air is blocked, it spreads outwards.

Igor tells us about the history of the Vernadsky base. A lot has changed since the age of balloons to measure the atmosphere. One of the main studies carried out is ionospherics, the study of the ozone layer which is in the ionosphere where 90 per cent of the ozone is found. The other ten per cent is in the stratosphere, but this is fairly insignificant. In 1985 the ozone layer was one of the main scientific areas being studied at this base by Joe Farman and Jonathan Shanklin when it was then the British base, Faraday. The instrument they used to carry out their studies was the Dobson spectrophotometer which was named after G.M.B. Dobson, one of the first scientists to investigate atmospheric ozone. The Dobson spectrophotometer is a spectral instrument which measures, records and transmits the measurement of matter. Igor is working on measuring the intensity of irradiation and wavelengths, using this intensity to calculate the thickness of the ozone. If the ozone thickness is low, then a lot of ultraviolet irradiation is transmitted to earth and vice versa. Chemical reactions intensify as temperature increases permitting more ultraviolet radiation to arrive at sea level.

While working at Faraday, Joe Farman, the chief scientist, and Jonathan Shanklin discovered the hole in the ozone layer purely by accident while working with the spectrophotometer. They were printing out a graph of their work to give to scientists in Cambridge when they noticed an anomaly. After investigating this ,they found a build up of chlorofluorocarbons (CFCs) trapped in a cloud during the Antarctic winter which had caused a hole in the ozone layer. It showed that one little chemical from spray cans and other sources was causing a very serious problem for the planet even though it was many miles up in the air. The build up of CFCs didn't happen during the Antarctic summer months.

With our newfound knowledge of the atmosphere we make our way to Igor's 'den' to see this important bit of equipment for ourselves. The spectrophotometer that Igor is working with is housed on the first floor which involves a climb up a vertical ladder fixed to the wall to get to it. Igor also sleeps up there in another room to the right. He tells us that all equipment at the station has a more personal, non-scientific name, always a woman's name. There is a generator named Clara, and the first Dobson 031 spectrophotometer was called Lupe. Igor is using more modern equipment; a new updated version of the Dobson spectrophotometer. I ask him what its name is and he tells me it hasn't got one yet. Then he asks me what my name is. I tell him it's Virginia, so he says that's what he'll call it and asks me to write it down for him. I think I'd rather have a penguin named after me than a machine! However, globally the spectrophotometer has a greater impact on our understanding of the planet and how to protect it. I'm very honoured to have such an important piece of equipment named after me. I'd love to know who Clara and Lupe were. I imagine it's more homely to say to your colleagues "Clara's playing up again," rather than "the generator's causing problems" or "Virginia's giving out a lot of important data. I don't know how we'd survive without her." Much better than that spectrophotometer!

I'm fascinated by what Igor is telling us about the ozone layer. Unlike oxygen and carbon dioxide, which are colourless and odourless, ozone is blue and has a distinctive smell. I am told it smells like geraniums. I remember my father telling me to inhale the smell of the ozone when we went on the beach sometimes at night. Does that mean there must be an ozone layer in the sea as well as the upper atmosphere? I'm not sure if what I could smell was ozone; it was probably dried seaweed. I ask Igor a lot of questions and admire his patience in answering them. It must be very difficult to explain such complicated scientific ideas in language that a lay person can understand, made doubly difficult for him as English isn't his native language.

What a lot to take in, but so interesting. The only reason for humans to live in Antarctica is to carry out scientific observations so that we can understand the world of nature better and hopefully protect it. This journey is not just about the thrill of gazing at gigantic icebergs, or watching the antics of birds and mammals, it is also about education. Although the word ozone has been part of my vocabulary since childhood, it is really something I know nothing about. That is until I meet Igor, now at least I'm slightly better informed and ozone is no longer just a word—it now has meaning and the important function of preventing the Earth from burning up.

The ionosphere is in the uppermost layer of the atmosphere, consisting of several distinct regions which extend from an altitude of about 40 miles (60km) and continue through the mesosphere and thermosphere to around 300 miles (480km). The ozone layer in this upper atmosphere is where the gas ozone forms its greatest concentration. It is formed as a result of the separation of molecular oxygen into single atoms by solar UV radiation, enabling them to join any unaffected oxygen molecules, producing the heavier ozone molecule. Ozone can absorb large quantities of harmful UV light forming a gaseous 'umbrella' surrounding the Earth, shielding it from extensive radiation and cosmic particles and also maintains balance of heat on Earth. This ozone layer consists of several different gases which include oxygen, nitrogen and carbon dioxide. It also contains water vapour. The oxygen content decreases with altitude and increased light. As the CFCs float up into the ozone layer they encounter stray ultraviolet rays that haven't been absorbed by the ozone. This 'collision' causes the CFCs to release harmful chlorine and they begin to multiply destroying thousands of ozone molecules.

We've all heard about the hole in the ozone layer and are aware that there is an increase in skin cancer due to this. However, many of us, including me, have little understanding of just how serious this is for the planet and all life upon it. The ozone layer sits in the lower part of the ionosphere, between 10 and 50 kilometres above Earth, where it blocks the sun's seasonal changes and also sporadic solar flares and coronal mass ejections (CME), which have the ability to seriously interfere with shortwave and satellite communications, and even terrestrial telephone and computer networks.

Ozone protects living things from dangerous UV-B radiation which can cause skin cancer, cell mutation, cataracts and immune system diseases. Crops are also being affected. In particular, phytoplankton, which forms the basis of the Earth's food chain, is very vulnerable to UV-B radiation. The hole in the ozone layer is thought to be caused by CFCs (and other ozone-depleting substances), which are man-made chemicals produced in modern industry and released into the atmosphere, breaking down the ozone. CFCs are chemicals used in refrigeration, aerosols, solvents and the production of plastics and foam. They are stable and not altered by natural agents such as rain, so they build up and then they are broken down by UV radiation in the upper layer of the stratosphere, resulting in the destruction of the ozone layer. It takes only a small amount of CFCs to destroy a vast amount of ozone. CFCs that are in the atmosphere now will still be there in 100 years time, and we keep adding to them. The depletion of the ozone layer and the resulting serious consequences to the planet led to the Montreal Protocol being drawn up. It was agreed in 1987 and is an international treaty to eliminate the production of CFCs and other chemicals that cause depletion of the ozone layer based on scientific data. It was ratified in 1989 by 197 states.

The Industrial Revolution was probably the genesis of climate change. Scientists have examined layers of snow in Antarctica and Greenland dating from the late eighteenth century, which show a marked rise in carbon dioxide and methane gases. Carbon dioxide levels have been rising steadily every year, by more than 30 per cent since the Industrial Revolution. Intensive agricultural methods have led to the release of nitrous oxide and methane, leading to climate change. The ice sheet reflects sunlight back into the stratosphere like a mirror, and chemicals build up in the winter months and are released when the sun returns. These chemicals are generated all over the planet, but there is a particular ozone 'hole' that is is concentrated over Antarctica due to strong circular winds over the continent known as the 'polar vortex'. Although natural forces such as solar cycles and volcanic eruptions play a part in the destruction of the ozone layer, humans are by far the most destructive force in causing changes to our planet. More broadly in relation to wider climate change processes, if things continue in this way, it will lead to sea levels rising; glaciers are already retreating, and permafrost is melting. Climate change affects average temperatures, and when raised lead to wetter weather and flooding and more intense storms in some areas, while other areas will experience droughts leading to the decline in agricultural yields and famine. The outlook isn't very encouraging.

Apart from the geophysical poles, in Antarctica there is the pole of inaccessibility which is the furthest point from all of the Antarctic coasts. The Russian base of Vostok is located here and it is the coldest place on the planet at -89°C. The ice sheet here is very thick. Scientists have managed to drill a core to a depth going back 400,000 years and retrieve ice containing bubbles of the Earth's ancient air enabling them to measure the levels of carbon dioxide. The resulting analysis of this ancient ice showed that over the last 400,000 years carbon dioxide levels had never been anywhere near as high as they are now. This discovery prompted scientists to dig back deeper to 800,000 years, to find the results were the same as the ice 400,000 later. The scientists discovered that at very cold temperatures the carbon dioxide was low, at warmer temperatures it was high proving that carbon dioxide was a major influence on climate. Levels of carbon dioxide have never been as high as they are now. Not far from Vostok Station is the South Geomagnetic Pole which is the centre for all auroral activity.

I have experienced so much in the way of nature, but I am totally unprepared for my experience of listening to Igor explaining the history and scientific work carried out at the base, giving me an insight into a new dimension that I previously had no idea about. What have I been doing all these years I've been on this planet? How many times have I gazed with pleasure at the blue infinity above me, or watched the clouds drifting across the sky forming wonderful shapes. Not once have I stopped to contemplate what is up there apart from the Sun, the Moon, stars, clouds and rain. The ionosphere is where meteors or shooting stars can sometimes be seen, zooming across the night sky at extraordinary speeds of up to 100km per second. What a revelation to know a little bit about what is 'up there'. It has become yet another new thing to wonder at. I can't thank Igor enough for the patience and enthusiasm he's shown in answering my naive questions, and also for the work he and other scientists are doing for the good of our planet.

Apart from all the very interesting and informative history of the base, Igor is also very open in expressing his feelings regarding the very different life in Antarctica compared to anywhere else on Earth. Mostly a stint in Antarctica lasts for about fourteen months or two years. For about seven months of the year they live without meeting other people, as ice prevents movement between bases and it's completely impossible for ships from the mainland to get to Antarctica during the almost continuous darkness and frozen seas of the winter months. Igor tells me that he isn't bothered by the 'cut off' existence, as it gives him more time for reading literature, listening to music, making sculptures in the snow and philosophising. He says he also likes to draw portraits in pencil of other base members at Vernadsky. It's lovely to hear about the human side of this very interesting man as well as the academic.

I think I'm getting in the way of myself and should move away from lofty science. The problem is that upper air physics is way above my head, excuse the pun. I think I'd better leave it to the experts.

Vodka

Following the weighty matters just discussed, I feel the need to balance this with a lighter more down to earth perspective which I hope will clear the air a bit. I'm not a scientist, I'm a grandmother, the woman next door. I live at 32 Any Street, Little Town, England. It's a small three-bedroom, semi-detached home with a small garden. The neighbouring homes are mainly the same as mine with just a few slightly larger detached ones. My neighbours are a mixture of white and blue collar workers. It's a typical suburban street where we all stop and chat to each other, usually about our families, holidays and the weather. We seldom socialise together except at Christmas when we have a neighbourly drink. My home life is a complete contrast from the 'home' at Vernadsky. I live at No. 32 but I have plummeted into another dimension at 65° south. A few days ago none of the passengers knew each other; in the case of the people at Vernadsky it was only a few hours ago we were all strangers. Now it feels as if we have been friends for a long time. Both 32 and 65°S are just numbers in different hemispheres. My neighbours and Antarctic friends are just people in different hemispheres, but all equally significant to me.

Despite rocketing high into the Earth's atmosphere and beyond, my feet are still riveted to the floor of Vernadsky base. Following in the footsteps of Aristotle and Ptolomy's idea that the world is in balance, I suddenly experience a new magnetic pull. From the higher plain of metaphysics and science I have a thirst of a different kind. As part of me floats in this new found world, the polar opposite is pulling me in completely the opposite direction, which is towards the bar and an hour of frivolity, fun and camaraderie between old friends and new, a glass of vodka firmly in my hand. At least the glass remains in my hand but the contents disappear out of the glass rather quickly. Where it's gone I can't imagine but I feel a lovely warm glow. I'm plummeted from the upper atmosphere to the down to earth trappings of the most amazing bar in the world. The bar at Vernadsky has the atmosphere of a small, very popular pub in a remote village where all the locals get together to unwind after a tiring day at work. Although we're just another ship load of visitors, complete strangers to the men working at the base, the Ukrainians are so friendly it feels as if we've known them for a long time. Everyone mixes in like old friends who have grown up together. The atmosphere is one of camaraderie and fun, it's hard to believe that the work carried out here is so serious and important to our knowledge of upper air conditions.

Now for more bragging rights: I am drinking in the first bar to

The Vernadsky bar

be opened at the bottom of the world! Not your usual local! The Ukrainians are wonderful hosts, so friendly and informative. The bar is adorned with an interesting array of paraphernalia, including flags of all nationalities, clocks, ornaments, foreign currency notes, soft toys, model ships, photos, and about six bras, one of which was extremely large—Lupe's maybe? Or possibly Clara's. Mine isn't worth having! We can buy postcards and stamps to send to friends and family, and there was a gift shop selling miniature penguins, and Ukrainian crafts and badges. What a difference a bar makes. Vernadsky is poles apart from the little gift shop and post office at Port Lockroy, but the latter is of historical importance, no longer a working, scientific base.

It is very much a party atmosphere—vodka shots, a pool table, interesting conversation and a shop that sells t-shirts, toy penguins, postcards and Ukrainian crafts. Some of my fellow passengers are playing pool, but I prefer to prop up the bar and chat. Also the feel of the vodka glass in my hand is very comforting. Kate and John, fellow passengers and now friends, join me at the bar where we spend a very enjoyable time knocking back shots of neat vodka followed by a slice of lemon dipped in brown sugar. I feel on top of the world, not at the bottom. I believe the expression is 'high as a kite' but in a very different way from the kites at the start of our afternoon at Vernadsky.

Kate and John are teachers and have taken a year out to travel round the world together. They met Ingrid our marine biologist while they were in New Zealand, and it was through her they came to Antarctica. It hadn't been part of their schedule, but Antarctic seeds seem to take root very easily in people. Like me, they couldn't envisage the impact it would have on them. I think it's having a far reaching effect on them, making the rest of the interesting and beautiful places they've travelled recede into the distant corners of their memory. Although Kate is younger than my two sons, we hit it off right from the start and know we'll keep in touch as they live in the next county to me, so within easy visiting distance. Kate has the cheek to ask Igor to call his spectrophotometer Virginia Kate. Obviously too much vodka!!

All too soon it is time to take our leave and say goodbye to our great hosts. Igor and I exchange email addresses. He tells me that during the Antarctic summer, they receive visitors from the British base of Rothera and Palmer USA station, both bases carrying out scientific research, sharing all knowledge with the other nations in Antarctica. A number of tourists 'explorers', like me also visit; all visitors come to Antarctica for peaceful reasons and education. Igor says that in his opinion, Antarctica is a place where you can meet only good, honest people. He's convinced that it can't be different. I tend to agree. For me anyone who visits or works in Antarctica becomes part of one big family in which trust is absolute. Reluctantly it's time to say goodbye to my new friends. The time seems to have passed so quickly, but it's time to move on to our next destination.

Wordie House and Pleneau Island

The Zodiacs take us through narrow channels to our next destination, Wordie House, just a short ride from Vernadsky. Wordie House, the building of the British base known as Base F, was built as a meteorology research station. The base was established on

Winter Island, in the Argentine Islands, at 65°S in 1947 by the Falkland Islands Dependency as Base F. The construction itself was named after James Wordie, a Scottish explorer who joined Shackleton's 1914 expedition to make the first crossing of the Antarctic continent. He was instrumental in establishing the base at Port Lockroy to guard British interests in Antarctica and in the formation of Operation Tabarin. He died in 1962, aged 72. The base closed in 1954 when the new base of Faraday (now Vernadsky) was established. Wordie House is now maintained by personnel from nearby Vernadsky.

The building is not much more than a hut and very cramped, as it had been built to house four to five people when it was a working base. It must have been a very lonely and difficult existence for the men who were stationed there for up to two and a half years at a time. It is now a museum of historic importance as it was one of the first bases established in Antarctica to study meteorology.

There are only two rooms: a bunk room with two bunk beds with rather musty-looking black and white striped mattresses on each bed, and a kitchen. There are drawers between the bunks, an old clock, a radio, plates and cutlery on shelves next to the bunks. The kitchen area contains a well-stocked assortment of culinary

Wordie House

178

The bunk room at Wordie House

delights such as Atora suet, Bird's custard powder and tinned food. There is no bathroom, only an old zinc tub in front of the stove which had to be filled by heating up hot water on the stove; it was the only way the men could have an occasional wash. There is a rather rusty looking boxed-in lavatory housed in a very small room next to the bunk room. Everywhere feels cold with only dim light penetrating through the small window panes. I find it hard to believe that up to five men could live here for several years with little contact with the outside world Living in such a confined space must have called for a great deal of tolerance and self-sacrifice. Compared with the other bases we've visited, Wordie House feels like a cold, unwelcoming hut that has a haunted feel to it. Interesting though it is, I'm glad when it's time to leave and feel the crunch of the snow beneath my feet and look at the multi-coloured sky and a colony of cormorants (antarctic shags) diving for their dinner.

We head back to the ship, and once aboard I have a moment of panic as I try to recall some of the information Igor has given me. My mind has gone blank as if a wave has washed over me taking everything out to sea. That may well have something to do with the vodka; I don't usually drink spirits, only wine. However, back in my cabin, key words shoot through the atmosphere in my head like shooting stars, I am able to write them down for researching further at a later date.

There is an unexpected announcement that in half an hour we will be going on an evening Zodiac cruise round Pleneau Island, and, surrounding icebergs, our final outing of the day. It was named after Paul Pleneau, a photographer on a French expedition in 1903. The sea is perfectly still, not even a ripple apart from the wake of the Zodiacs. Like our evening visit to Cierva Cove in the early part of our journey, it was like an ice garden with crabeater seals lolling on small icebergs and leopard seals frolicking round the Zodiacs. Despite these similarities, the area around Pleneau Island is completely different; the area of sea is far more open with icebergs of all sizes and shapes dotted around like statues in a museum. There are also white and blue glaciers tumbling down from the high basalt rock cliffs. The deep crevasses are an electric, gleaming blue with veins of different colour variations. The Sun is

Inspecting ice sculptures around Pleneau Island in the Zodiac

still shining showing no sign of going down for the night. It is as if it wants to enjoy the moment too. At Cierva Cove it was much later in the evening when we set out, and night was falling when we went back to the ship. Once again I'm lost in time and the 'now'—it's a lovely feeling. However, our two chefs are shut away in the galley preparing our end of day dinner, the Slavic theme lingering over from the vodka is not over yet.

There's just time for a hot beverage while we chat excitedly about our day's experiences so far. The vodka and atmosphere at Vernadsky, and the Zodiac cruise has given us all a healthy appetite for tonight's Russian dinner. What can we expect this time? It wouldn't surprise me if a troup of cossack dancers materialised over the side of the ship–this journey is so full of the unexpected. However, we've had enough entertainment for one day both serious and fun, now the focus is on food. Our Chilean chefs have never let us down yet, but neither Russia or Ukraine are noted as being the top countries in the world for their cuisine. Time will tell!

Dinner is served. Wondering what culinary delights await us, I open the menu. It's a bit like opening a present and won-

Mesmerising shapes in the water

dering what on earth can be inside. On the inside cover there's a small painting of the Kremlin and 'RUSSIAN DINNER' written above it. Below are the words 'PRIJTNOGO APPETITA', no prizes for guessing what that means. The wine list features wines from France and Argentina. On the opposite page is the main menu which starts with a choice of appetizers which are *morskoy briz* or *borch* (in English, borsch or borscht). I've heard of the latter which is traditional vegetable soup (usually including beetroot) with sour cream. That sounds delicious. I'm intrigued by *morsky briz*, but can't quite bring myself to order it without knowing what it is. I'm told it is Russian-style seafood salad. Decisions, decisions! There are salads and dressings on the buffet so I plump for *borch*. The main course called OCEAN is *krasnaija riba*—grilled salmon on basil sauce, served with beetroot rice and spring onions. EXPLORER is stroganoff (easy), beef stew with beetroots, gherkins, mushrooms and green peppers, served with potato cubes. ANTARCTIC is *gallupsi*—stuffed cabbage roll served with carrot sauce. I can't decide whether to have OCEAN or EXPLORER. I go for the salmon. DESSERT is *khleb* pudding with vanilla sauce. Nobody seems to know what exactly that is so I play safe and have fresh fruit from the buffet. The whole meal is delicious and I'm sorry our Russian experience has come to an end. I can feel another childhood dream taking hold, a journey on the Tran-Siberian Railway from Moscow to Vladivostok, but I think it will be a long time before I build up my courage to do it. For some strange reason when I was about twelve years old, my geography teacher at school made us learn all the stops on the Trans-Siberian Railway for homework. I was quite happy to do it as my sister and I used to try and reel off all the names of the stations from Havant to Waterloo station, and see who could do it the fastest but without missing a single station out.

Libby tells me that it's only another 60 nautical miles to the Antarctic Circle between the Penola Strait and Lemaire Channel at 66°S. I don't know if it's the vodka that is affecting us, but in a fit of childlike spontaneity we go and ask the captain if we can go there. Unfortunately he tells us that it's impossible as it would add another three days to our journey. In land miles 60 seems like nothing, but we are on a small ship not in a fast car on a motorway. Of course the weather can also be a problem, particularly as we are only a few weeks away from the onset of winter, we could be held up even longer if the weather takes a turn for the worst. Like some of the past explorers, we might be forced to overwinter in the ice. Much as I love Antarctica, I also miss my family. It was worth a try asking him.

17. CRESCENDO AT DAWN

"At home I am used to seeing the sun leap straight out of the east, cross the sky overhead, and set in a line perpendicular to the western horizon. Here (Antarctica) the sun swings to a different law. It lives by extremes ..."
Admiral Byrd, *Alone*

We are woken by Geoff's warm, friendly voice; it's a comforting and familiar alarm call. It reminds me of being woken up in the morning by my mother or father when I was a child. I have the same trust in him that he will take good care of us on our amazing journey that I'd had for my parents. That sounds very silly as I'm old enough to be his mother, but then age is just a number, not a reality: feelings are real. It's 7.00am—just enough time to nip to the bar for a cup of coffee, and a croissant. Sipping my delicious warm coffee, I gaze out of the window at the early morning light. Just above the horizon the dawn is beginning to spread a gentle, misty light across the sky, sweeping the night time clouds away. I am in a dream world as I watch a pale glow of light peep over the orb of the Earth, then creep stealthily along the wall of the horizon as if trying not to be noticed.

Just like Admiral Byrd, one of the things I find very strange in the southern hemisphere is the movement of the sun. I remember when I was working in Santiago, Chile, I went to look at an apartment to rent. There were six separate blocks of flats well spaced out, some had six floors, some ten floors. They were set in extensive gardens so didn't give a feeling of being crowded together. The thing that particularly appealed to me was the barbecue area next to a lovely big swimming pool. Perfect, I thought. It was located in front of one of the apartment blocks which meant it faced south. It would get the sun all day as there were no buildings immedi-

185

ately to the east or west, or in front of it. At 11.00am one morning I went down to the pool at to have a swim and sit in the sun for a while. I couldn't believe my eyes when I got there; the pool was in complete shade. Then I twigged. In the southern hemisphere the sun rises in the east, but goes round to the north before setting in the west. I suddenly realised that I'd become so used to the movement of the sun back home, that I was no longer conscious of it. It wasn't easy trying to adjust to such a complete contrast from what I had always taken for granted. It made me realise that I should wake up and take more notice of everyday things around me. My experience and revelation of the Sun's movement in the two different hemispheres makes me understand Admiral Byrd's feelings and need to write about it.

Time to stop day dreaming and get ready for our 7.45am landing on Cuverville Island at 64°41'S. It was named after J.M.A. Cavelier de Cuverville, a vice admiral in the French navy. This is probably going to be our last landing on our incredible adventure as we are back in the Errera Channel, heading nearer to the northern tip of the Peninsula and the Bransfield Strait, soon to be followed by the dreaded Drake Passage; a crossing that no one is looking forward to.

By now everyone is in the routine of flipping their tags and disinfecting their boots. It has become second nature. Also, very importantly, we've got used to lathering on a high factor sunscreen lotion. I thought this was totally unnecessary at the beginning of the trip and frequently didn't bother. I couldn't understand how sun, which didn't seem to have any strength in it especially in such a cold climate, could possibly cause skin damage. I thought that only happened when you got sunburnt and that wasn't likely to happen. How wrong I was! I'm told the story of a BAS scientist who went out skiing without putting sunscreen on. He returned to base in agony with a very livid, sore red face. It seemed even less necessary in the evenings. As I learn more and more about Antarctica and the hole in the ozone layer, I realise just how important it is, even in the evening when we are out cruising round icebergs. My thanks are due to Martine, a fellow passenger, who is also a medical doctor. She always carries a tube of sun-screen in her pocket which she generously hands around to ignorant passengers like me. As we zoom towards Cuverville Island the sky is beginning to brighten up, the hazy sun has plucked up the courage to climb just above the horizon and is glinting on the glistening white and blue ice castles. It looks just as the poet Samuel Coleridge described in a scene in *The Ancient Mariner*:

The ice was here, the ice was there,
The ice was all around
It cracked and growled, and roared and howled
Like noises in a swound.

These Antarctic icebergs never fail to give me a sense of wonder and enchantment. We are starting with an iceberg cruise, mainly growlers which are bergs that have rolled over when the sea has melted the ice underneath the berg causing it to become top-heavy. Our Zodiac driver, Shane, points out the features to look out for that indicates an iceberg is likely to roll in the near future. We stop next to a perfect example and Shane points out the prominent top-heavy arches and deep blue cracks. The berg in question is very still and silent, as if the very thought of toppling over is beneath its dignity. Somehow it looks very stately and secure in its grandeur. I could happily spend most of the morning just gazing at its majestic beauty: it has a meditative effect on me. From one angle it looks like a pyramid with blue ribbon woven into it and a shelf like a ballerina's skirt swirling out on the waterline. Below that the ice seems to taper away, like the lower part of a humming top which is bathed in blue light. From another angle it's a fairy-tale castle with turrets and pinnacles along the top.

With cameras still clicking, we speed away to look at another incredible berg not far away. It starts with a low throaty growl followed by a creaking sound like the hinges of a door. Suddenly the low, throaty growling sound rapidly becomes a thunderous roar. We turn to look in the direction the sound is coming from just in time to see the berg we were previously looking at topple over with an almighty splash. What a crescendo to finish on! For its curtain call it bobs about for a short time like a performer in the theatre bowing to thunderous applause, before regaining its

Melting ice, all around, about to topple

equilibrium, leaving itself and the sea as calm as if the performance has never taken place. It's so thrilling, I almost think I've imagined it. Of course I know I haven't as it's the talking point for everyone as we land on the volcanic sand and pebble beach of Cuverville Island.

188

Penguin rush hour

Penguins are becoming as commonplace as people in a city. We've always been surrounded by penguins on every landing, but this is the penguin Tokyo of Antarctica. There are far more than I've ever seen before. I have a bizarre image of a few penguins pushing all the others into a railway carriage in rush hour. It's a flash back to my first day of going to work by train during rush hour in Tokyo; it was like nothing I'd ever encountered before, just a sea of black and white movement. Of course it was black-haired men in dark suits, white shirts and gloves, not unlike penguins in their appearance, pushing us all onto the trains, but somehow all these black coated penguins have triggered the memory.

As usual they waddle over to greet us and then seem to act like tour guides of their island. They peck at our boots and trouser legs as if telling us to follow them. One grabs hold of Audrey's (one of the passengers) scarf and tries to pull her along. One gives us a demonstration of how to build a nest. She keeps picking up peb-

Playful penguins with whale vertebra, en masse in background

bles in her bill and placing them in a stone circle on the ground. Sadly though, I'm told that she has probably lost her eggs or chicks to a skua and her maternal instincts are telling her to try again. Of course it's far too late in the season as all this season's chicks have almost fledged and will be off, taking to the sea before the big freeze takes over. I feel quite sad as I think about how I'd feel in that situation. Although penguins may not have quite the same emotions as humans, nevertheless they obviously care about the safety and life of their offspring. I'm sure they experience a strong degree of emotional pain if an egg or a chick is snatched by a predator.

The beach is littered with whale bones of all shapes and sizes. I take a photo of a penguin looking through the hole of a large vertebra; it's like a picture framing its face. There's another using a bone as a pillow to rest its head on. I walk to another part of the beach where some of our group are sitting on rocks, watching the antics of some penguins testing the water. The penguins are standing on a rocky outcrop on the edge of the beach; they remind me of children daring each other to jump in and clamber out again—it's lovely to watch as they seem to be having so much fun. Penguins often stand on the edge of rocks or ice before jumping into the water. None of them want to be the first to jump straight off into the jaws of a hungry leopard seal lurking below the surface. I am fascinated by the torpedo-like speed in which those in the sea zoom out onto a landing site often having to clear quite substantial heights. Their ungainly waddle on land is in such complete contrast to their streamlined grace in the sea. They can spend hours in the water but their airborne time is a matter of seconds. Their speed is phenomenal given that their wings, or flippers, don't enable them to fly, unlike most other species of bird. Instead they have very dense feathers that seal out water and trap air in the downy feathers in an under layer at the base of each shaft. This is made up of microscopic filaments that trap air next to the body that acts like a jet engine propelling them at great speed through the water and onto quite high ice or rocks. Suddenly there's a commotion and thrashing in the water. Like a flash of lightning a leopard seal grabs one of the penguins by its feet as it's standing on the edge of a rock. The seal takes the poor little thing out to sea a short way and starts shaking it violently and thrashing it against the surface of the water. Its wings flap frantically for ages as it appears to be trying to get away. Then the seal submerges with the penguin for a while before popping up again. It continues to shake it, its wings still flapping, but it's probably dead at this point so the movement is just due to the violent shaking. It must be a horrific death and is certainly very upsetting to watch. However, it's also very interesting to see raw nature in the wild. At least seals only kill to eat, not for greed, power or hatred like some species of 'animals' I could mention. Seals shake their victims like mad to get them out of their extremely thick skins, so they can get to the flesh. They need to eat at least seven penguins a day to survive. Life and death are never far apart in Antarctica.

As I walk back towards the waiting Zodiacs, I feel very sad, as if I've just been to a funeral. It makes it all the more poignant when I see fellow passenger, Thorfin, sitting on the beach with his long legs stretched out in front of him, a gentoo penguin sitting on his lap gazing up at him like an adoring domestic animal. Penguins are not just a species of bird, they've become our friends and they all have quirky personalities.

Gentoo penguin —
personality included

At 10.00am we set off in the Zodiacs to look at the glacier lined coast, and more icebergs. There's something pink floating in the water. Ingrid, our Zodiac driver, cuts the engine to just ticking over as we head slowly towards the object. It's the carcass of the penguin, the remains of the leopard seal's breakfast floating in the water. A subdued silence descends on us all as we see the gory remains of a little creature that not long before we'd been watching playing in the icy water with its friends. All that was left was its head, which was intact, its large webbed feet and its quite small skeleton with a few pieces of pink flesh still attached to it as it floats on the surface of the water. The heartbeat of Antarctica remains indifferent; bergy bits float calmly by, the ice continues to roar and howl, and the other penguins continue their games as if nothing has happened. An interesting experience, but very sad. I don't think there's a lot of flesh on a penguin. Their fat looking bodies are mainly thick blubbery skin and very tightly packed feathers, insulation rather than flesh.

On the return journey to the ship Alex is my Zodiac driver. Keeping a safe distance, we gaze at a large piece of a glacier that looks as if it's about to calve off. We wait a while, willing it to happen, but it refuses to oblige. I suppose two show-stopping performances in one morning is too much to ask for. We move on to a very spectacular iceberg with spiky ice pinnacles along one side. They rise into the sky like gleaming spires on a cathedral. Perched on the top of each spire, like a beautiful statue on a pedestal, is an Antarctic tern; very graceful birds with a forked tail, often called sea swallows. They have white under bodies with silver-grey backs and wings, a black cap on their heads and bright red bills and feet, they weigh between four and seven ounces. Antarctic terns are very agile flyers and have an average life span of up to 30 years. They remain in Antarctica all-year round unlike arctic terns which just spend the austral summer months in Antarctica, then fly to the Arctic for the northern hemisphere summer, making a round trip of 44,000 miles a year; the longest migration known. Researchers estimate that Arctic terns migrate about one and a half million miles over their lifetime. That is approximately equal to three return trips to the moon.

I find it incredible and almost inconceivable that such a tiny,

Antarctic terns on ice pinnacles

graceful bird has the strength to make such a long journey twice a year. An Arctic tern weighs between three and a half and four and a half ounces, with a wingspan of just over two feet. I think they are my favourite bird. I don't know how long it takes them to make this extraordinary, marathon journey. Earlier I talked about human endurance. I think the birds of Antarctica also need to be recognised for their endurance. I wonder why arctic terns need to spend six months of the year in the southern hemisphere and six months in the northern hemisphere. Why can't they take a feather out of the Antarctic tern's book and stay in one or the other hemisphere? Perhaps they're more daring and adventurous, or maybe there's a greater abundance of food during the Arctic summer. Sadly we have to leave this fairy-tale iceberg castle and head back to the *Shokalskiy* for sustenance. It is sad because it also heralds the end of our time in Antarctica, a land which has seen so much in its long life as an independent continent.

Back aboard ship I tuck into a hearty brunch of scrambled eggs, bacon, sausages, croquet potatoes, muesli with orange juice, yoghurt and fresh fruit. This is followed by pancakes with maple syrup. I'm surprised the ship doesn't sink!. But that might be a significant effect on appetite of the pure, embracing Antarctic air. After brunch we are told to listen out for announcements regarding expedition plans for the afternoon.

Shrouded in the mists of time

As we continue our journey up the Errera Channel, I go up to the bridge and see minke and humpback whales. Minke whales are one of the smallest of the baleen whales at 20–35 feet long. They eat krill, cod and herring. They mate between December and May and the gestation period is about ten months. They can hold their breath under water for up to 20 minutes, but normally stay under for much less than that. They are the only baleen whales still commercially fished. I don't know what their numbers are, but I presume stocks are being carefully monitored.

It's getting very foggy as we sail into Wilhelmina Bay and the Melchoir Islands. We are still quite a long way from the Antarctic Convergence, but winter is rapidly approaching. I spend most of

The *Shokalskiy* becomes shrouded in mist

the afternoon on the deck or the bridge as I'm very aware that our time in this fascinating part of the world is rapidly coming to an end. I want to make the most of what little is left. I make occasional sorties to the bar for coffee and biscuits and a chat with fellow passengers. Some people are already starting to download some of their photos onto the computer in readiness for them to be included in the group CD the leaders are putting together; they are going to give us all a copy as a reminder of our expedition. It's a lovely idea that I hadn't expected. At long last we get an announcement to say we are going on our final Zodiac cruise of the expedition. I have a mixture of emotions; pleasure because I love being out near the ice and wildlife, mixed with sadness because it's the end of what has proved to be a life-changing experience. I don't want it all to end, I love zooming off to explore new territory in these Antarctic wilds, and the knowledge that this will be my last time is hard to accept.

As we make our way down the gangplank to the waiting Zodiacs, thick fog is rolling in like a blizzard of mist rather than snow. Visibility is low, the atmosphere is creepy rather than completely enveloping like it was with the blizzard. Maybe because in the fog we can see eerie shadows and just an outline of coast; with the blizzard there was nothing but bright whiteness. Not long after speeding off in the Zodiacs, the *Shokalskiy* is lost in a dull white misty shroud. I wonder how our drivers will be able to find her again but I know I have nothing to worry about. Although visibility is low, we are able to see a lot of fur seals lying on some rocks. We enter a shallow stretch of water near an Argentinean base. The water is crystal clear and we can see a beautiful starfish lying on the sea bed. Ingrid, our marine biologist, also points out what looks like tiny grains of white rice in the sea; to my surprise she tells us they're krill. Without her pointing them out, I'd never have realised they were living marine creatures, part of the very basis of the food chain. It makes me realise that even the smallest, most insignificant looking creature has an influence on the lives of every living creature on earth which includes us. Without krill the food chain would collapse, leaving us to starve along with other animals and plants, all of which we rely on. Before coming to Antarctica, I saw a television programme about the proposed development of an island in the Indian Ocean. Conservationists were against it, as the reef around it contained rare wildlife. The developers were disgusted that the conservationists were putting such rare life as sea cucumbers above humans. Unfortunately the arrogance of humankind will be our downfall, but it may well be too late to save the planet as well.

A lone blue-eyed shag, a member of the cormorant family, is watching us with interest. Perhaps he's thinking we are going to eat his dinner. They live in colonies around the northern tip of the peninsula close to sheltered water. They have white bellies and black heads and backs. At a glance they could be mistaken for a penguin, but they have much longer necks and wings. They can also fly, unlike penguins. Their eyes are a beautiful blue, hence their name. They dive several metres underwater in search of food and remain in Antarctica for as long as there is open water, and then they migrate as the sea freezes over, returning when the ice melts.

One of the Zodiacs stops at the shore for passengers to look at a glacier. When it's time to leave, the start cord won't work. The other Zodiacs speed over to offer help. That's the first and only time that we've experienced any technical difficulties with equipment. Shane, Zodiac driver extraordinaire, manages to get it going just in time to whisk the occupants back to the ship in time for an early dinner. I can't see any sign of the ship anywhere in the vicinity, but the Zodiac drivers seem to have a special sense which the rest of us mere mortals lack. Perhaps it's the same sense as a homing pigeon or bee.

After dinner Geoff warns us that we are heading back to the Drake Passage and suggests that it might be a good idea to go and see Drew, our ship's doctor. He very kindly dishes out phenergan tablets like a benevolent Father Christmas to stop seasickness. I decide to take some even though I still have several ear patches left. They didn't stop me feeling sick crossing the Drake Passage on the way out to Antarctica, they just made me very sleepy, so it is worth trying something else. However, I've since been told that you are more likely to be seasick in a fairly calm sea, if there's a swell, than in a very rough one. At this point I'm not aware of what the wind and sea conditions will be like on the way back, so decide to err on the side of caution. Prevention is better than cure even though I'm sure I've got my sea legs by now and have become a hardened sailor who can cope with any extremes that nature throws at me.

We all go to the bar after dinner as the icy dark fingers of the rapidly approaching Antarctic winter start to grip the sky and the sea. There's nothing to see from the bridge but blackness, the sea and sky merging to make one continuous black canvas. There isn't even a hint of the moon or stars to give a glimmer of light. How different it is from the beautiful, translucent sky we gazed at just a few days ago in Cierva Cove. The bar is a very welcoming place and there's always so much to talk about. Although we've always zoomed off in Zodiacs to the same place together, it doesn't mean we all see or experience the same things either in transit or on land. We are always free to wander off on our own and look at things of interest, or simply to sit in silence absorbing the new world around us and getting to know the 'locals'. There's so much to talk about at the end of a day in Antarctica and so much enthusiasm to compare our experiences with each other.

After such a long day, a lot of us drift off to bed at around midnight. Every evening someone turns the covers back on the bed and puts a 'good night' chocolate on our pillows. On the wrapper it has a polar bear in the top right hand corner, and a penguin in the bottom left hand corner. It's a lovely touch from Quark Expeditions, whose care and service is faultless. So, it's back to a night of sliding up and down as we head back across the Southern Ocean.

18. THE SCREAMING SIXTIES

"An Antarctic expedition is the worst way to
have the best time of your life."
Apsley Cherry-Garard

Our position is 60° 54'S, the barometer has gone up and the wind
and sea speed measures nine on the Beaufort Scale; strong gale
force winds of 47–54 miles per hour, and precipitous seas with
waves of 35–40 feet. All doors leading out onto the decks are
bolted shut as it is far too dangerous to even poke your head outside. The ship is rolling so heavily that all presentations have been
postponed.

At 4.00pm I go up to the bridge to watch the mountainous
seas. It's almost impossible to stand upright, even when clutching
hold of the railing with both hands. Several times I get thrown
across the room. Well, that's a bit of an exaggeration; I lose my
balance and fall over a few times. We are well and truly in the
screaming sixties. I love it! The incredible power and energy of
nature is forcing the water into a roaring mountainous wall that
is rising up with the speed of a whale breaching, its roaring battle
cry becomes a shriek as each wave is succeeded by a larger wave
that breaks with a thunderous crash over the decks and smashes
against the widows of the bridge with ferocious power. As if
ashamed of its outburst, the foaming fury falls back to the lowest
deck and slides sheepishly away into the icy foaming depths of
the waters below, completely spent like naughty children who've
just played a dangerous prank on their unsuspecting victims and
run off before they can be reprimanded. Then the next wave will
follow with just as much rage. Anything that isn't bolted down
goes flying. I now know why it has the reputation for being the
roughest sea in the world! Well this crossing proves that I have

The Screaming Sixties – not a photographer's dream

become a hardened sailor, ready for anything; I have my sea legs and don't feel sick at all. In fact I'm on an adrenalin high and love every second of it. Once again I have complete trust in the crew, who I have nothing but praise for. I'm completely mesmerised by the thunderous sea and stand rooted to the spot—that is unless I'm being flung to the side by a sudden lurch. I keep thinking, "Just one more massive wave and then I'll go down to the bar." One more becomes another and another. I simply can't tear myself away. The sea is amazing to watch. I am like a child riding on a rollercoaster, screaming with excitement from time to time. I want another go, then another.

At 5.50pm I manage to tear myself away from this mesmerising, thrilling spectacle and go to the bar for a pre-dinner drink. Suddenly there's an almighty crash as a lot of glasses slide onto the floor behind the bar. Angela, the hotel manager, and Rijan, the head waiter, calmly take it all in their stride as if it is an everyday occurrence. Obviously for them it may not happen every day, but certainly it must happen quite regularly. Libby joins me and we decide we'd better have some red wine before the bottles go flying too. Fortunately they don't. It's a good excuse for an apéritif before dinner, and a relaxing chat with our other fellow passengers who haven't succumbed to the usual horizontal position adopted by many of us in rough weather, and for some in not such rough weather.

Not many people make it to the dining room for dinner. I can't believe how well I'm feeling. I totter to the buffet and get some soup but find it impossible to carry it and stand upright; I need two hands for the ship. Rijan to the rescue, he carries it to the table for me and sets it down. He does so with such aplomb without spilling a drop or falling over. I'm very impressed! No sooner has he put it down and turned away, than it goes flying along the table top and slops over despite the non-slip tablecloth. I give up on the soup after trying to scoop it off the table and put it back in the bowl by now it's cold anyway. I wait for the main course and just manage to carry that myself without depositing the contents of the plate on the floor, or worse still all over my neighbour sitting at the table. I'll have to come back as an octopus in my next life. It's almost impossible to eat anything, if you don't hold on to your plate and cutlery, everything slides along the table. Fortunately nothing falls off on the floor as the table has a raised edge around it like a tray and the tables and chairs are bolted to the floor. If we hold onto our plates and such, then we can't hold onto the table, which means we slide off our chairs like dominoes, knocking everyone else over and ending up in a heap on the floor; it's like a comedy sketch. Very little food makes it into our mouths and stomachs. The musical accompaniment during dinner is the rousing sound of cutlery and crockery crashing to the floor in the galley. Just like Angela and Rijan in the bar, the two chefs calmly continue with their culinary skills as if it's a normal dinner time occurrence.

It is midnight and most of us head off to our cabins wondering what adventures we'll have while trying to get some sleep. I have no problem staying in my bunk as I'm sleeping thwart ships, but I feel as though the gigantic waves are having a tug of war with me. One moment my head is propelled into the side of the wardrobe, the next my feet rebound off the opposite wall. I'm glad the porthole isn't immediately at the foot of my bed otherwise I might slide through it into the foaming depths. I don't think I'd find the precipitous sea so exciting if that happened. I expect it's firmly bolted shut like everything else on the ship that gives access to the raging outside world.

I haven't slept well and anyone who says they have is obviously lying! The ship has been rolling and groaning all night, but it doesn't bother me as it's all part of the adventure. I'm also aware of how lucky I am to be in quite a spacious, centrally heated cabin in an ironclad ship that was built specifically for polar waters, and with an engine not sails.

Once again my mind goes back to the explorers who in the past had sailed into this unknown territory in wooden sailing vessels, often succumbing to scurvy and frostbite through lack of good food. Many of them never returned home but perished in the freezing temperatures. In some cases their bodies have never been found; they lie in terra incognita under deep snow and ice, or at the bottom of the ocean. We have the luxury of an air ambulance that will lift us from the ship and take us to the nearest hospital in an emergency.

Earlier I said that Scott and his four companions had all died by the end of March 1912. It took nearly a year for their bodies to be found and the news of their deaths to reach their loved ones. What can I say? I doubt that anybody could even remotely feel they can understand what it must have felt like. I wonder what motivates people to carry out such extreme activities, putting themselves in the jaws of death; parting from loved ones knowing you may well be saying goodbye forever. As Shackleton put in his advertisement for men for his Endurance voyage, "SAFE RETURN DOUBTFUL". It is bad enough saying goodbye when you are going off on an expedition in the safety and comfort of a modern ship which is built to go through ice, and you have warm clothing, good food, communication services and stringent safety precautions. My experience of Antarctica has been so amazing. My extreme contrast of comfort and safety compared to that of past explorers induces shivers to run up and down my spine. I know I haven't been anywhere near the South Pole, nor have I had to walk miles across really dangerous terrain, but I feel guilty that

I've had it so good, when others died in such atrocious conditions so far from home.

We are out of Antarctic waters, the Antarctic Convergence and the screaming sixties, and into the furious fifties. Yesterday the *Shokalskiy* was doing 9 knots; today we're doing 13 knots. We have covered 260 nautical miles in the last 24 hours. Our valiant little ship must look very vulnerable being swamped by waves of almost the same height as the top most deck of the ship. I don't particularly like being on the sea, I'd rather be in it if it's calm, but at no time have I ever worried that it might disappear beneath the waves. I would willingly go through the experience again. Antarctica is worth it! As Apsley Cherry-Garrard said, 'it's the worst way to have the best time of your life.'

Sadly we are reminded that our incredible journey is nearing its end. There's a lull in activities, no more precipitous waves, only rough seas similar to ones I've often seen before. There are very few sea birds or wildlife of any description. I wonder where the wandering albatrosses are as they spend most of their lives at sea. I go to my cabin to start packing and catch up with writing in my journal. I don't get anything done as I end up chatting to Libby whose intention it is to start packing too. We succumb to finishing up the remains of the last bottle of wine that I brought on board for use in the cabin. I don't really want to pack as I don't want the journey to end. Once again I feel myself slipping back into childhood when anything is achievable if it's what you want; that means I can't think that this journey will really end until I want it to. If I don't start packing, then the journey will continue. My journal is important to me as it's my personal record of my journey. I'm sure most of it will be imprinted in my memory forever, but little details tend to get forgotten, and I know from past experience that the next adventure tends to dim the lights of the previous one. It seems hard to believe that is possible at the moment, but time will tell. I'll let you know after my Trans-Siberian-Kamchatka expedition.

At 11.15am we both go to the lecture room to watch Alex's talk and pictures, 'Field work in Antarctica: a glaciology grunt's perspective'. He gives us a picture of his life as a glaciologist and the type of work he carries out. Where have I been living all these years I've been on this planet? Despite having travelled extensively and experienced a very varied life and career, I am now aware of how little I know about this incredible world we live in. Not just the world but career prospects open to people. When I was at school we didn't learn anything about geology or glaciology. However, even if I had known about such careers, I probably wouldn't have wavered in my passion to be a ballerina. "Childhood dreams"! I did manage to make a living in the theatre but not in a ballet company unless one week in London City Ballet's production of *Giselle* at Chichester Festival Theatre counts.

After lunch I feel I really have to make a start on my packing. I hate leaving everything to the last minute. I manage to get quite a bit done and then decide that my time would be better spent on the bridge watching out for whales and birds. My decision is the right one. I see black-browed albatrosses - they are relatively easy to identify as they have a distinctive facial pattern. They look as if a make-up artist has painted a black brow above their eyes. Their bills are bright orange or yellow with a reddish tip. They have a wingspan of just over eight feet. We are also graced with the company of a wandering albatross. It is beautiful to watch it soaring into the sky, then skimming downwards into a trough of waves,

The bridge of the *Shokalskiy* in quieter seas

then rising sharply into the wind its wings forming a graceful, shallow arc.

While I'm on the Bridge I have my photo taken with Captain Kiselev. The part of my personality that forms my theatrical nature wants a picture of the captain with one hand on the steering wheel and the other arm round his girl, me, as he negotiates the ship's passage across storm tossed waters. I don't think he quite understands the image I want, but he probably has better things to do with his time than watch low-grade movies where the tough guy can courageously maintain the stability of the ship in tremendous seas, while at the same time find it possible for a bit of romance with an adoring woman. Mission accomplished, well nearly, he has one arm round me but the other hand isn't on the steering wheel, it is holding onto a cabinet that houses a radar screen. I dread to think what I'll be like when I'm 80.

We will only save what we love

The effect the polar regions have on the planet as a whole is hard to realise while we are sitting in our centrally heated homes and offices, blaming the unusual weather conditions on anything but ourselves. The easiest thing to do is to bury our heads in the sand, or preferably a holiday brochure and decide which sunny climate to jet off to. Yes, I'm just as guilty as everyone else! However, I'm much more aware of my carbon footprint now and am trying to do as much as I can to lessen climate change. Most of us, including me, know very little about how the Poles affect us. We hear so many conflicting opinions about causes of climate change it is hard to know what we can really do to prevent it. How do we know who to believe? Scientists do not always agree it would appear. I recently bought a book entitled *Merchants of Doubt* and the following is a quote from the back cover: "*Merchants of Doubt* was one of the most talked-about climate change books of recent years, for reasons easy to understand. It tells the controversial story of how a loose-knit group of high-level scientists and scientific advisers, with deep connections to politics and industry, ran effective campaigns to mislead the public and deny well established scientific knowledge over four decades. The same individuals who claim the science of global warming is 'not settled' have also denied the truth about studies linking smoking to lung cancer, coal smoke to acid rain, and CFCs to the ozone hole. 'Doubt is our product', wrote one tobacco executive. These 'experts' supplied it. Greed and self-interest are powerful incentives, so manipulating scientific finding is all part of the game."

Nobody could have predicted the speed at which the ice caps are melting. I have seen it first-hand with a glacier that I first saw in 2005 in Ushuaia. It was already gradually receding and just three years later the glacier had retreated a fair distance further. That is frightening! The current situation regarding the conflicting opinions about the planet is expressed very succinctly with minimum words by Baba Dioum, 'For in the end we will save only what we love. We love only what we understand. We will understand only what we are taught.'

Baba Dioum is a Senegalese environmentalist and this quote comes from a speech he made at a meeting of the International Union of Conservation of Nature in 1968. I can fully understand how difficult it must be for desperately poor countries whose only means of survival is to grow crops that are changing the environment to the environment's detriment. That is the only way they can put food on the table—for many people on our planet, to stop production would mean their livelihood would be threatened. How can they care about the environment? They must save what they love: their families. Even rich nations do not really appear to be bothered about the effects modern society is having on the environment. They make the right noises but can't seem to put their money where their mouth is. Simply breaking a few habits of a lifetime and cutting back on energy might sound easy initially, but making adjustments to one's lifestyle is more difficult than one would think, even when you are genuinely concerned. It's much more comfortable to get in a car to go even a short distance than it is to walk, particularly when it's raining.

Despite feeling so strongly about the planet and now being so much more aware of the importance of conservation, I still find it hard to change the lifestyle I'm accustomed to. I have changed a number of things such as riding my bike or walking whenever I can. I recycle things and conserve water by using the water I've washed fruit and vegetables in on the garden. I've also bought two rain butts so I don't need to use the hose very often. It all sounds very simple, but it's quite time consuming and requires forethought. How true Baba Dioum's words are; 'We will save only what we understand.' I love the planet because I have been taught to understand it, in more depth. I have not been indoctrinated into this understanding; it has come through increased knowledge and my own experience, very little of which I had even a rudimentary understanding of before. I feel very concerned when I see pictures of extreme weather patterns across the globe and the destruction, loss of life and despair these events cause. I know that nature is playing a part in climate change, but we are hastening it at a dangerous speed. I feel very guilty and hope that the little bit I am doing may be helping. I suppose anything is better than nothing.

Sadly our last day is drawing to a close. Dinner is a quiet affair —plates don't slide up and down, nobody falls in a heap on the floor, and it's possible to walk around with just one hand for the ship. We then gather in the lecture room for the final event on our journey. We are given a copy of the *Students on Ice Information Handbook* which contains a lot of interesting information about Tierra del Fuego and Antarctica. My experience and this volume together were the catalyst that inspired me to write this book. I have gained so much that I want to share my experience with other people who are interested in Antarctica. Those of us who were brave, or foolish enough, to swim in the cold Antarctic waters— which was most of us—are given a certificate of bravery for joining the prestigious 'Polar Plunge Club'. The next event should have been introduced with a drum roll. It is our joint effort slide show which reflects the beautiful scenery, wildlife, the passengers and leaders who have been like a family, and some hilarious moments. We have all contributed some of our photos to be transferred to a CD and we are all given a copy as a keepsake—a lovely idea. After viewing over 300 pictures I think we all feel at a loose end, or lacking any positive direction. Our automatic pilot steers us to the bar to share our thoughts and experiences, and to have a few farewell drinks. After consuming more than is good for us (though it is a special occasion), at around midnight we go on deck as we

enter the calm waters of the Beagle Channel. It's good to be out
in the fresh air after being held prisoner during our screaming
sixties crossing. The sea is as calm as a millpond. It is as hard to
believe that just a few hours earlier we were rollercoasting in precipitous seas. We can just make out the coastline of Cape Horn in
the moonlight. The *Shokalskiy* drops anchor and we wait for the
pilot boat to guide us up the Beagle Channel to Ushuaia. I relect
upon words I read in the *Students on Ice Handbook* that resonate:

> Antarctica is certainly not as remote as it once was and that's
> why it needs protecting more than ever before, it's remoteness
> is no longer going to save it. Antarctica is a place that will be
> with us all forever, we will continue to draw on our experiences
> and memories, and go forth as protectors and advocates for
> this very special place on earth.

19. EL FIN DEL MUNDO

We arrive back where we started

I wake up at 6.30am to the sound of Geoff's voice giving us our wake up call for the last time. I get up straight away and look out of the porthole. It's still dark, but a pale watery light is just visible on the eastern horizon. The twinkling lights of Ushuaia are sending out a lovely welcome home message as they shimmer in the steadily falling rain, casting pools of coloured light in the puddles on the quayside. As the dawn spreads silently along the Beagle Channel, it casts its early rays on the mountain tops, which are providing a stunning backdrop now that the peaks are covered in snow. Winter is on its way here as well as in Antarctica. When we left eleven days ago, there was very little snow on the mountains except for the highest ones.

Despite the early start to the day there's a hive of activity as everyone is up and about. There's last minute packing to do before making our way to the dining room for our last breakfast on the *Shokalskiy*. The atmosphere is subdued, partly because there's an air of sadness in saying 'sayonara' (goodbye in Japanese) to such a memorable experience, and partly because a good number of us are suffering from a hangover. Many haven't been to bed. Normally the dining rooms are filled with lively conversation, but not this morning. It's as if we're strangers. Our disembarkation time is 8.30am so after breakfast it's time to say goodbye to new/old friends. It's hard to believe that this life I've shared with so many interesting people has come to an end. In some ways the eleven-day expedition has flown by, but in others it seems to have always been a part of my life. It's like the end of an era. The only thing I can compare it with is when I was a dancer in the theatre and the final curtain came down on the last night. There were usually tears as we took off our costumes and wiped off our make-up. Would we

209

ever meet again, or do any more shows together? I wonder if I'll ever see any of the people from the *Shokalskiy* again, apart from the ones who are going back to the Antarctica Hostel. The walk down the gangplank onto the quayside is lonely and final, every step hesitant knowing that when I set foot on the quayside I won't see my cabin again. I want to run back and hug everybody one last time. I expect the crew are relieved to see the back of us, they've probably been tossed around on the Southern Ocean for about five months and soon they'll be heading back to Vladivostok to see their loved ones. For them it's a leap from the southern hemisphere autumn, to the northern hemisphere spring.

By the time I've said goodbye a hundred times, the rain has eased a little so I decide to walk back to the hostel, enjoying the fresh air rather than getting a taxi. The empty streets of Ushuaia are just beginning to come to life with traffic and people emerging like bedraggled butterflies from a chrysalis. I find it quite difficult to walk along the pavements in a straight line, and feel as if the ground beneath my feet is moving. Is it an earth tremor? I've experienced them many times while I was living in Japan, and Chile is also on a tectonic plate and part of the Ring of Fire prone to earthquakes and volcanic eruptions. I realise though that I'm suffering from 'dockrock'. It often happens when you've been at sea for a while and got your sea legs. When you get back on land, you have to adjust to the lack of motion and this can cause a kind of reverse seasickness. Fortunately it's very mild and I find it quite amusing; at least it's another new experience. To passers-by I probably look just a little tipsy. We can't get into our rooms till midday, so there's a bit of a morning party atmosphere; at least amongst those who are sober enough to be conscious and coherent. The hungover bodies snoring on the sofas are totally oblivious to life around them. They remind me of inert seals lolling on ice floes; although seals at least have their eyes open and are ever watchful of their surroundings. These have their eyes shut but their mouths open. The Sun has decided to join the party, but prefers to stay outside the window and look in bathing the room with warm light.

I take my rubber boots and waterproof trousers back to the hire shop in the town. Having wondered if I'll ever see any of my fellow passengers again, just three hours after disembarking I bump into fellow passenger, Mike. He's standing at the top of the stairs in the shop and calls out to me. It sounds ridiculous but I'm so pleased to see him and that he's real, not a figment of my slightly inebriated imagination. In fact there are several other people in the shop who were on the *Shokalskiy*, all returning their gear. They're staying in a hostel not far from mine. We suggest trying to get as many people as possible together for a spit-roast dinner in the evening. I suppose we're all reluctant to let go of the experience we've enjoyed together. Also most of us are travelling alone so it's nice to be with other people for dinner. When I return to the hostel I tell the others about it as soon as they are conscious. There are six Antarctica passengers from the *Shokalskiy* staying at the Hostel Antarctica; everyone is enthusiastic about having a final dinner together, so it's going to be another big reunion farewell party after all.

In the early evening I'm in a party mood, I have a bottle of wine in my locker that I bought and didn't drink before I left for Antarctica. I go and get that and buy another bottle of wine from the bar. Marianne opens the bottles and I invite her to join us for a drink. As she's about to go off duty, she agrees. We have quite a party as, apart from the six passengers from the *Shokalskiy*, we are also joined by other residents who've been on a different ship. The bottles are emptied very quickly so Marianne buys another.

We've arranged to meet at 7.00pm There are about eighteen of us at the restaurant including the two Chilean chefs, Drew, the ship's doctor and Marilyn, the professor of economics. The wine flows easily as does the conversation and laughter. I'm enjoying the evening very much and probably have a lot more wine than is good for me, but who's counting? In the centre of the restaurant there's a big spread of various salads and hot vegetables. The spits for the meat are located in a big window just to the right of the entrance to the restaurant. The roasting meat is lamb and beef which is sizzling away on long, vertical spits over glowing red hot embers. They are certainly enticing the customers in. Chefs are carving as many slices off the meat as the customers want. There's no limit to how many times one can go back for more. Alcohol is the only thing not included in the price, but a bottle of wine is very cheap compared to England. I eat enough food to sink a battle ship, but Argentinean lamb and beef is the best in the world in my opinion.

As the wine flows I suddenly remember back to my first evening in Ushuaia and my night out with Darren at the king crab restaurant; in a light-hearted moment of madness and intoxication I go up to one of the waiters and tell him that it's Drew's birthday. About ten minutes later a cake with one candle is placed in front of him and everyone sings Happy Birthday. The look of bewilderment on his face is a picture! Everyone thinks he's a dark horse keeping his birthday a secret. Looking very confused he says 'It's not my birthday.' I have to tell everyone the story of Darren. The laughter is a lovely ending to a great evening. We have shared such an amazing experience which I know will live on in all of us.

20. EPILOGUE

"It is the duty of an explorer to bring back something more than a mere account of his movements. He must take every advantage of his unique opportunity and add to the edifice of knowledge those stories which can only be qualified in the regions he visits."
(Robert Falcon Scott)

Since returning to England I've kept in touch by email with quite a lot of my fellow passengers and the expedition leaders. I really appreciate their support and encouragement in writing this book. I have kept in touch with Kate who lives in the next county to me. Libby comes to the UK from South Africa every winter to work; we always try to find time to spend a few days together. It's lovely to reminisce and look at photos together and talk about our new adventures. With others, I've kept in touch by email.

I have also made a new friend who wasn't on the *Shokalskiy* with me, Steve Norris. My local newspaper wrote an article about my expedition to Antarctica, which included my occupation and place of work. Steve was so impressed by my enthusiasm for Antarctica that he wrote to me at work. He is very different from the group of people I became so close to during my Antarctic adventure. My new friend had spent some considerable time in Antarctica, but not as a tourist. As a young man he had worked in Antarctica for several years at a time. His life-changing journey began in 1973 when he'd just got back from travelling in the USA and Canada. He was an electrical engineer by profession and he saw an advertisement in a newspaper for electrical engineers to work in Antarctica for two and a half years. He applied and went to London for the interview. It took place in an old Victorian building, but he can't recall where. He was walking along a corridor when he encountered a man trying to put up a tent. The man said to him, "Grab hold of this rope please, it's got to stand up to 100 mile an hour winds in temperatures of -40°". Steve of course obliged. A bit later he was called into a room where to his amazement one of the three interviewers was the man who'd been trying to put up the tent. It was none other than the explorer, Sir Vivian Fuchs. Interview over he was asked to wait in another room. Eventually Sir Vivian came out and told him he'd got the job. He went to Cambridge for lectures and training. In August 1973 he sailed from Southampton to the Falkland Islands on the RRS *Bransfield*. From there he went to South Georgia and down the eastern side of the Antarctic Peninsula, eventually ending up at the British Base of Halley on the eastern side of Antarctica for a few months. He helped in the construction of the base and told me the following amusing anecdote. He said that they had to dig a toilet pit 30 feet deep and 6 feet by 6 feet square. Then they built the walls and roof of the building and a bench-type seat to sit on. There were two separate cubicles divided by a thin wall, each with a hole in the seat. During the construction nobody had taken into consideration the logistics of the distribution of solid matter dropping into the pit. As the faeces fell to the bottom of the icy pit, they froze solid very quickly in temperatures of -40°C which meant they piled up to form a pyramid that eventually reached almost to the top of the lavatory. They became known as 'turdi-cles' and the only way to remove them was by lowering men into the pit to saw and chop them down. As they were chopping they frequently got chippings in their mouths. Steve also said that it wasn't much fun having to drop your trousers in such tempera-tures. How the other half live!

After this he was back to South Georgia again, but he asked for a transfer back to Halley in 1974/5 and from there he went to another British base, Rothera, which is on the western side of the peninsula, south of the Antarctic Circle. Then it was back to the UK again. He hadn't been back long when he got a phone call from the British Antarctic Survey offering him the position of Senior Electrical Engineer on the RRS *Biscoe*; this time it was ship-based work in Antarctica. His work finished in 1981 just six months before the start of the Falklands War. When he returned to England he got married and went to live and work in the Far

East and Oman. He got a further offer of work in Antarctica as Senior Engineer on RRS *Bransfield* from January 1994 to December 1999. He lives very near me and has become a very helpful, interesting and good friend. We often go to London together to listen to presentations at the Royal Geographical Society. I also accompany him to the Annual General Meeting of the South Georgia Association every year.

Since my return to England, Igor Gvozdovskyy, my guide at the Ukrainian base of Vernadsky and I have kept in contact by email. He told me that exactly a year after I visited Vernadsky, he officially named the spectrophotometer 'Virginia'. I felt really honoured to have some little part of Antarctica bearing my name. When I told him I was writing a book about my experience, he sent me the following letter as he thought I might like to use it in my book. It's his translation from Ukrainian into English of a letter he sent to a friend in the Ukraine while he was working at Vernadsky. Although there are a few grammatical errors, I thought it was such a beautifully written, emotive letter that I have decided to include it without any correction. The errors in no way detract from the descriptions and emotions of the text—if anything they add a touching picture of the man himself, a man who is prepared to put a lot of effort into translating it into a foreign language.

I did not think that you will be impressed by a fly on the moss. I visited here in travel some place where I found more mites, red spiders the size of approximately 1mm. A last days I have immersed in a microcosm of Antarctica. Snow suddenly melts, open places with moss and lichens. After ozone measurements, it is from 21–00 to 00–30, in the last days I go to those places and sit down beside them, and three hours just looking at that green, rest, and think about many things ... I think that cells of my brain is filled only positive. Near a grass there is the smell of soil, but I understand that grass grows not on soil but on something similar to the soil. But is the smell? ... Or is it a simply olfactory hallucination? Snow descends and somewhere formed streams that flow and I like listen to these nice sounds as early spring in Ukraine. It is romanticism! In the sun the snow is changed to the drops of water, which can be observed on the mosses and grass. Drops are like diamonds, which is scattered across this green carpet and sparkle in the sunlight. Or these drops can be compared with the morning dew in the summer in Ukraine. And you now believe that in life nothing more to them this beauty and wealth, which gives you this Antarctic nature. All your wealth is here and there, displayed in your brain. From this awareness sends shivers down my spine owing to a positive impression. What a contrast! You and this Antarctic nature – all this is the contrast of extremes! Towards night, the temperature gets lower and drops turn into crystals with very strange and irregular shapes. In the sun, which comes crystals are real treasures that are made by nature. Crystals are like jewellry. In the sun, which comes over the mountains and the horizon crystals are real treasures that are made by nature. Crystals are like jewelry gold. And I well know that if tomorrow will be the sun, then everything will repeat itself. I am leaving this place with hope that I will return here tomorrow again. It is hard to let go this green car-

Ice crystals as photographed by Igor himself

pet and babbling streams, all these diamonds and gold, my good and nice thoughts, my bright children's dreams, although I know that they will not be fulfilled. I am very hard let go of Antarctica. It is possible never. Do I need to do it/ Of course, there is no need ...

Igor and I have remained in touch by email, he has since married and has two children. I think this is such an emotive piece of writing it is hard to write anything worthy of following it; but it is hard to stop writing about Antarctica and perhaps the following is a fitting way of ending my Antarctic experience for the end is also the beginning.

One hundred years on, our great explorers are still very much in the public eye and remembered for the work they carried out which has led to our greater knowledge of the planet. I get a comforting feeling when dates of significant events in Antarctic history coincide with dates in my life. Is it serendipity that these things happen?

On 29 February 2012, I went to an exhibition at the Royal Geographical Society with my friend, Helen, entitled 'With Scott to the Pole'. It was a leap year, the previous leap year I was in Antarctica just beginning my incredible experience. On 29th February 2008 I made my first landing in Antarctica on HO Island, South Shetlands; but it was very different from that of 100 years ago. One hundred years ago on 29 February 1912, a group of men were experiencing a very different Antarctica from mine. They were the six men who travelled with Scott and were called the Eastern Party. They had headed north to Cape Adare for six weeks to chart the terrain and carry out scientific work but had been forced to spend two winters on the ice. One hundred years ago today, the story of those six men who'd faced such an unimaginable ordeal, their extreme hardships of lack of real shelter, food and very debilitating sickness were very vivid in my memory. I am standing in a warm room surrounded by people chatting, a glass of red wine in my hand as I walk around the exhibition looking at the old black and white photos and reading the diaries of the men who gave so much for their country and our greater understanding of the planet. I feel honoured to be there to remember them, but very humbled by their courage and endurance. Their life would have been unendurable, but they managed to survive.

It is 29 March 2012; I am making my final entry in this book. I have just returned from a very moving Antarctic experience. This morning I attended a service at St Paul's Cathedral to commemorate the centenary of the British Antarctic (Terra Nova) Expedition, 1910–13, led by Captain Robert Falcon Scott CVO, RN.

Steve and I travelled to London by train. It was very early in the morning, the Sun had been up for about an hour and a half. As we travelled through the beautiful Hampshire countryside I looked at the verdant rolling hills, the primroses lining the railway banks, the daffodils standing upright and proud, the rabbits were nibbling the juicy grass that was still glistening with dew. The new green leaves bursting from the trees had that soft, tender glow like the skin of a newborn baby. Although it was only five days into official springtime, the sky was a vast expanse of cloudless blue stretching to infinity. The temperature was already in the high teens. I thought about Scott and his four men and what they would have been experiencing at this moment 100 years ago. Blizzards, frostbite, starvation and death; an extreme contrast from my experience today. I felt tears prick the back of my eyes to the point that I quickly had to focus my mind on something else as I didn't want to make a fool of myself in front of all the other passengers. I thought about my granddaughter who'd just won a medal in a gymnastics competition despite being the youngest entrant.

St Paul's Cathedral was such a fitting place to hold this commemoration service, its grandeur was a symbol of the grandeur of the Antarctic mountains and icebergs. It was also a statement of the stature of the men we were commemorating. I feel so honoured to have been part of this service and to be able to have shared in the experience of being part of a special group of people who came together as one in this hallowed place to remember Britain's Antarctic heritage and these brave men. The first commemoration reading was given by Sir David Attenborough. This was followed by a reading by Falcon Scott, the grandson of Robert Falcon Scott; and the second lesson was read by HRH The Princess Royal. It was a very moving and beautiful service and once again tears weren't far away as I felt they were all 'family'.

Although my story is an account of my movements, I have also given an outline of more than just what I did and the places I visited. I hope by writing this book I'll be helping to protect this unique continent and also be encouraging people to go there and just switch off and absorb the incredible, timeless surroundings. Limited tourism is good as it spreads the message that Antarctica needs protecting. Also the wildlife is stringently monitored to check what effects, if any, tourism has on the 'natives'. The more people understand the message, the better. As Chief Seattle suggested, if we all lived in the knowledge that we are just another strand in the web of life, just passing through, of no more importance than anything else on the planet, then the world would be a better place for all living things.

The bragging rights of joining the 'Polar Plunge Club' are a great conversational point, but are only the outward show. The knowledge I've gained, the amazing wildlife I've encountered, including the cruel side of nature, the awe-inspiring scenery, the kindness and enthusiasm of all our leaders on my incredible journey through Antarctica and the friends I've made have given me an inward purpose that has become part of me and will remain with me forever. The value of life is not money, possessions or beauty, but memories and a sense of connectedness. It is these things that have caused me to make a remarkable reassessment of values. As Baba Dioum said, 'We will save only what we love and we will love only what we are taught and understand'. I love Antarctica, I love our planet, but only because I now understand more clearly the uniqueness of everything on Earth and how everything is dependent on everything else.

Scott's diary had been retrieved and on 29 March 1912, on that day he made his final entry in his diary:

Had we lived, we should have had a tale to tell of the hardihood, endurance, and courage of my companions which would have stirred the heart of every Englishman. It seems a pity but I do not think I can write more. These rough notes and our dead bodies must tell the tale. For God's sake look after our people.

Through reflecting on his remarkable legacy my final words are similar, 'For God's sake look after our planet.'

Afterword

Antarctica makes a tremendous impact upon visitors, as it did for Virginia Bazlinton. However, during her journeys, Virginia also made an impression: her name and the date of her first Antarctic visit in 2008 were engraved on the Dobson Spectrophotometer at the Ukrainian Base on the Argentine Islands exactly a year later in 2009—and gave rise to this charming book—two most remarkable events.

Alan Carroll, Historical Adviser to the United Kingdom Antarctic Heritage Trust, erstwhile Base Leader at Port Lockroy from November 1954 to March 1957; awarded the Polar Medal in 2008.

LIST OF ANTARCTIC WILDLIFE

BIRDS

ANTARCTIC BLUE EYED SHAG (*Phalacrocoraxbrandsfieldensis*)
ANTARCTIC TERN (*Sterna vittata*)
BLACK-BELLIED STORM PETREL (*Fregetta tropica*)
BLACK–BROWED ALBATROSS (*Thalassarche melanophris*)
CAPE PETREL (*Daption capense*)
COMMON GIANT PETREL (*Macronectes giganteus*)
CRESTED CARACARA (*Caracara plancus*)
GREY–HEADED ALBATROSS (*Thalassarche chrysostoma*)
KELP GOOSE (*Chloephaga hybrid malvinarum*)
KELP GULL (*Larus dominicanus*)
LONG–TAILED MEADOWLARK (*Sturnella loyca falklandica*)
MAGALLANIC WOODPECKER (*Campephilus magellanicus*)
RHEA (*Rheidae*)
SNOW PETREL (*Pagodroma nivea*)
SNOWY SHEATHBILL (*Chionis albus*)
SOOTY SHEARWATER (*Puffinus griseus*)
SOUTHERN ANTARCTIC FULMAR (*Fulmarus glacialoides*)
SUB–ANTARCTIC BROWN SKUA (*Stercorarius lonnbergii*)
WANDERING ALBATROSS (*Diomedea exulans*)
WHITE–CHINNED PETREL (*Pterodroma mollis*)

PENGUINS

ADELIE PENGUIN (*Pygosclis adeliae*)
CHINSTRAP PENGUIN (*Pygoscelis antarcticus*)
GENTOO PENGUIN (*Pygoscelis papua*)
MACARONI PENGUIN (*Eudyptes chrysocome*)

MAGALLANIC PENGUIN (*Spheniscus magellanicus*)

SEALS

ANTARCTIC FUR SEAL (*Arctocephalus gazelle*)
CRABEATER SEAL (*Lobodon carcinophaga*)
SOUTHERN ELEPHANT SEAL (*Mirounga lionina*)
LEOPARD SEAL (*Hydruga leptonyx*)
SOUTH AMERICAN SEA LION (*Otaria flavescens*)

WHALES

ANTARCTIC MINKE WHALE (*Balaenoptera bonaerensis*)
FIN WHALE (*Balaenoptera physalus*)
HUMPBACK WHALE (*Megaptera novaeangliae*)
ORCA (*Orcinus orca*)

ANIMALS

GUANACO (*Lama guanicoe*)
PATAGONIAN GREY FOX (*Dusicyon greseys*)

PLANTS
CALAFATE (*Berberis buxiifolia*)
LENGA (*Nothofagus antarctica*)

Acknowledgements

I would like to thank the following people for their help and support in writing this book. Without their encouragement it would not have come to fruition. In particular I must express my fulsome gratitude to Geoff Green our expedition leader for making our journey to Antarctica so interesting and informative. His enthusiasm for Antarctica and desire to ensure all the travellers got as much pleasure from the journey as possible was heart-warming. It is thanks to Geoff that I have been inspired to write this book. Also my gratitude to Alan Carroll, the advisor to the United Kingdom Antarctic Heritage Trust, for all the advice and help he has so willingly given me and proofreading the chapters on the UKAHT. My deep-felt thanks to Sir Ranulph Fiennes for kindly writing the foreword and in addition to Andrew Lockett, my publisher whose belief in me as a writer has helped shape the book. Igor Gvozdovskyy has my huge appreciation for his interesting guided tour and naming the spectrophotometer Virginia and his contributions to the book included in the text and pictures. My thanks to Ceri Tipler, friend and former colleague who has encouraged me and given support in the writing of *Forty Shades*. My deep gratitude to the expert leaders on the expedition—Alex Taylor (glaciologist), Belinda Sawyer, (polar adventurer and deep sea diver), Ingrid Visser (marine biologist) the late Juan Mazar Barnett (ornithologist), Marilyn Waring (world renowned political economist and ecologist), Captain Norman Baker (explorer, man of adventure), Shane Evoy (expedition leader and Zodiac driver) and Susan MacGregor (physicist and the oldest woman to overwinter at the South Pole). And also thanks to Steve Norris, my new Antarctic friend whose polar anecdotes never fail to cause laughter, Captain Stuart Lawrence who provided added information about the Antarctic Convergence and Rachel Morgan, former director of the UKAHT. I also must salute Camilla Nichol the new director of the UKAHT, Libby Stark – my cabin mate whose travel stories are endlessly entertaining and Jamie Owen for organising permission to use the picture of the Endurance stranded in the ice. I would also like to thank Nicola Perry for her encouragement and belief in me, and my friends who have given their time to read my manuscript and give vital criticism – Caroline Miller, Marianne Campbell, Alan Walker, James Harfield, Sarah Bone, Sheila Manning, Kate Roberts – and Helen Claxton-Roper.

Credits

p. 56 Extract from *Savage Luxury: The Slaughter of Baby Seals* by Brian Davies, (Souvenir Press, 1970).

p. 67 and p. 109 Extracts from *Alone: The Classic Polar Adventure* by Admiral Richard E. Byrd, ©1938 by Richard E. Byrd, renewed 1966 by Marie A. Byrd, afterword ©2003 by Kieran Mulvaney. *Alone* was originally published G.P. Putman's sons. Original text design by Paul Johnson. Reproduced by permission of Island Press, Washington DC.

p. 92 'Birth of Antarctica' a NASA image, reproduced courtesy the MODIS Rapid Response Team at NASA GSFC.

p. 94 'Composite mosiac image' reproduced courtesy the National Snow and Ice Data Center, based on data from NASA's Aqua and Terra MODIS sensors.

p. 127 The *Endurance* image reproduced with permission of Royal Geographical Society Enterprises.

p. 151 Extract from *Studies in Zen* by D.T. Suzuki (2013 edn) reproduced courtesy of Martino Publishing.

p. 205 Extract taken from the cover of *Merchants of Doubt* by Naomi Oreskes and Erik M Conway, used with permission ©Bloomsbury Publishing PLC.

Images p. 84 and p. 216 reproduced with kind permission of Igor Gvozdovskyy

All other images ©Ginni Bazlinton.

The author and publisher have made every effort to identify the source of material quoted at significant length in this book. If despite these efforts any attribution is missing or incorrect this will be corrected on any subsequent reprint if brought to the publisher's attention.